CompTIA Security+ Certification Study Guide

Network Security Essentials

Ahmed F. Sheikh

Apress®

CompTIA Security+ Certification Study Guide: Network Security Essentials

Ahmed F. Sheikh
Miami, FL, USA

ISBN-13 (pbk): 978-1-4842-6233-7   ISBN-13 (electronic): 978-1-4842-6234-4
https://doi.org/10.1007/978-1-4842-6234-4

Managing Director, Apress Media LLC: Welmoed Spahr
Acquisitions Editor: Susan McDermott
Development Editor: Laura Berendson
Coordinating Editor: Rita Fernando

Cover designed by eStudioCalamar

Cover image designed by Freepik (www.freepik.com)

Distributed to the book trade worldwide by Springer Science+Business Media New York, 1 New York Plaza, New York, NY 10004. Phone 1-800-SPRINGER, fax (201) 348-4505, e-mail orders-ny@springer-sbm.com, or visit www.springeronline.com. Apress Media, LLC is a California LLC and the sole member (owner) is Springer Science + Business Media Finance Inc (SSBM Finance Inc). SSBM Finance Inc is a **Delaware** corporation.

For information on translations, please e-mail booktranslations@springernature.com; for reprint, paperback, or audio rights, please e-mail bookpermissions@springernature.com.

Apress titles may be purchased in bulk for academic, corporate, or promotional use. eBook versions and licenses are also available for most titles. For more information, reference our Print and eBook Bulk Sales web page at http://www.apress.com/bulk-sales.

Any source code or other supplementary material referenced by the author in this book is available to readers on GitHub via the book's product page, located at www.apress.com/9781484262337. For more detailed information, please visit http://www.apress.com/source-code.

Printed on acid-free paper

This book is affectionately dedicated to all IT experts, professionals, and students.

Table of Contents

About the Author

Ahmed F. Sheikh is a Fulbright alumnus and has earned a master's degree in electrical engineering from Kansas State University, USA. He is a seasoned IT expert with a specialty in network security planning and skills in cloud computing. Currently, he is working as IT Expert Engineer at a leading IT electrical company.

About the Technical Reviewer

Asad Ali is associated with High Speed Networks Lab, National Chiao Tung University, Taiwan, since March 2018, where he is working on a research project funded by the Ministry of Science and Technology, Taiwan. In this project, he is designing a secure and federated authentication mechanism for multiple computing paradigms in collaboration with multiple partners in Bangladesh, Turkey, and the United States. He is also working on the cost minimization of bidirectional off-loading in federated computing paradigms. In the past, he has worked with the Network Benchmarking Lab (NBL), Taiwan, where he designed various security tests for IP cameras. He has various publications in the domains of Computer Networks, Cognitive Radio Networks, PCB Routing, Optimization, Internet of Things, and Network Security.

CHAPTER 1

General Security Concepts and Trends

In this chapter, we will review the goals of an information security program, and you will be introduced to the information security model, a three-dimensional model, which will be the foundation for learning the concepts of confidentiality, integrity, and availability.

By the end of this chapter, you will be able to

1. Identify the concepts of confidentiality, integrity and availability.

2. Perform packet-level analysis.

Information Security Model

In 1991, John McCumber created a model framework for establishing and evaluating information security (information assurance) programs, in what is now known as **The McCumber Cube**. This security model is depicted as a three-dimensional cube-like grid composed of information security properties or desired goals, information states, and safeguards.

1. **Desired Goals**: The first dimension of the information security model is made up of the three information security properties. The three desired goals include confidentiality, integrity, and availability. Use the acronym **CIA** to help remember these three principles.

    - Confidentiality prevents the disclosure of information for unauthorized people, resources, and processes.

© Ahmed F. Sheikh 2020
A. F Sheikh, *CompTIA Security+ Certification Study Guide*, https://doi.org/10.1007/978-1-4842-6234-4_1

- Integrity ensures that system information or processes have not been modified.

- Availability ensures that information is accessible by authorized users when it is needed.

Chris Perrin, IT Security Consultant, provides insight on the importance of being familiar with the industry standard term, CIA.

2. **Information States**: Data can be stored on a hard drive and can also be transmitted across a network or the Internet. Data can also be processed through manipulation by software. The second dimension of the information security model consists of processing, storage, and transmission.

3. **Safeguards**: Technology is usually what most information technology (IT) professionals think of when contemplating solutions to the information security puzzle. Policies and procedures provide the foundation for an organization. How would you know how to configure your firewall, a technology-based solution, without the proper policies and procedures to guide you? Educating employees through security awareness training program is an absolute must so that the security measures implemented within an organization are effective.

Everything that you learn about information security can be related back to one of the cells of this three-dimensional model.

Operational Model of Computer Security

The operational model of computer security is composed of different technologies. Protection is the sum of prevention (like firewalls or encryption) plus measures that are used for detection (like an intrusion detection system, audit logs, or honeypot) and response (backup incident response or computer forensics).

Protection = Prevention + (Detection + Response)

Prevention: Access controls, firewalls, and encryption

Detection: Audit logs, intrusion detection, and honeypot

Response: Backup incident response, and computer forensics

Diversity of Defense

In order for security to be effective, controls need to be implemented at different levels (Figure 1-1). For example, an organization may have a security guard monitoring the perimeter, and they may also require a biometric palm scan before entering the server room.

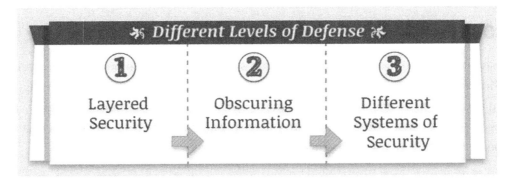

Figure 1-1. *Different Levels of Defense*

1. **Layered security** provides the most comprehensive security. Limit access to reduce threats; if attackers can penetrate one layer, diversity ensures that they cannot use the same method to penetrate other layers.

2. **Obscuring information** can be a way of protecting it. If an attacker does not know which operating system is running on a device, he cannot determine its weaknesses as easily.

3. **Different systems of security** such as keeping a system simple from the inside but complex from the outside can be beneficial.

3

Communications Security

Communications security is comprised of several subcomponents:

- **Cryptosecurity**: Cryptosecurity is the component that ensures that cryptosystems are sound and being used properly.

- **Transmission Security**: Transmission security measures protect transmissions from interception.

- **Physical Security**: Provides the physical measures that safeguard classified equipment, data, and documents.

- **Emission Security**: Includes measures taken to prevent an unauthorized person from intercepting or analyzing emanations, or the electronic signals that a device may produce.

Access Control

Access control defines a number of protection schemes which can be used to prevent unauthorized access to a computer system or network. Many devices can be configured with an access control list, or an ACL, to define whether a user has certain access privileges. Just because you can log onto the corporate network does not mean that you have permission to use the high-speed color printer.

Authentication

Authentication verifies the identity of a user. The subject needs to produce (1) a password, (2) a token or card (i.e., a badge), or (3) a type of biometric such as a fingerprint.

Authentication involves access control which deals with the ability of a subject (individual or process running on a computer system) to interact with an object (file or hardware device). If you go to an ATM for cash, you need your bank card which is considered something you have for which you need to know the PIN. This is an example of multifactor authentication or requiring more than one type of authentication. The most popular form of authentication is the use of passwords.

Social Engineering

Social engineering is the art of convincing an individual to provide you with confidential information. No technology is required here, just the gift of gab. The success of social engineering plays on the fact that most individuals in the business community are customer service-oriented and do their best to be of assistance. Remember, the weakest link in the security chain of a company is its people.

What is social engineering?

- It is the process of convincing an individual to provide confidential information or access to an unauthorized individual.

- It is one of the most successful methods that attackers use to gain access to computer systems and networks.

- It exploits the fact that most people have an inherent desire to be helpful or avoid confrontation.

- It gathers seemingly useless bits of information that, when put together, divulge other sensitive information.

Security Trends

The level of sophistication of attacks has increased, but the level of knowledge necessary to exploit vulnerabilities has decreased. The sheer volume of attacks is increasing, and for most organizations, it is not a question of if, but when. As the popularity of mobile devices increases, so does mobile malware. Think about the recent popularity of social networks. It does not take very long for a technology to become popular followed closely by ways to exploit the vulnerabilities associated with the technology.

Be aware of the specific types of attacks that are on the rise:

- Unauthorized access

- Phishing

- Bots on network

Due Care and Due Diligence

When looking at the steps taken to safeguard an organization's environment, due care and due diligence are two terms that come up and are connected (Figure 1-2).

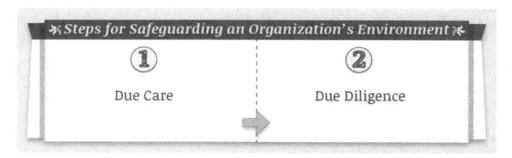

Figure 1-2. Steps to Safeguard an Organization's Environment

1. **Due care** looks at the steps an organization takes to protect the company, its resources, and its employees by having policies and procedures in place.

2. **Due diligence** requires that management have continual activities to ensure that protective measures are maintained and are operational. The standard here is one of a "prudent person." Would a prudent person find the activities appropriate and sincere?

Summary

The goals of an information security program include the foundational concepts of confidentiality, integrity, and availability. These three principles are aspects that comprise the framework of the information security model. In this lesson you learned about different levels of defenses and the importance of access control. Stay informed regarding the latest security trends to help prevent security vulnerabilities associated with technology.

Resources

- **Information Assurance**: https://searchcompliance.techtarget.com/definition/information-assurance

- **CIA Triad**: www.techrepublic.com/blog/it-security/the-cia-triad/488/

- **McCumber Cube**: www.captechu.edu/blog/learning-language-of-cybersecurity

CHAPTER 2

Network Fundamentals and Infrastructure Security

In this chapter you will gain an understanding of network fundamentals needed to understand network security, and you will also learn about security zones. Being familiar with the basic network architectures and protocols is the first step. Understanding other routing and address translation will help you to further understand the vulnerabilities and threats that can be exploited.

By the end of this chapter, you will be able to

1. Explain the security function and purpose of network devices and technologies.

2. Implement secure network administration principles.

3. Differentiate network design elements and compounds.

4. Use common protocols to employ infrastructure security.

5. Identify commonly used default network ports.

Network Architectures

Technology is filled with acronyms, and network architecture is no exception. The following acronyms are commonly associated with network architectures (see Figure 2-1):

© Ahmed F. Sheikh 2020
A. F Sheikh, *CompTIA Security+ Certification Study Guide*, https://doi.org/10.1007/978-1-4842-6234-4_2

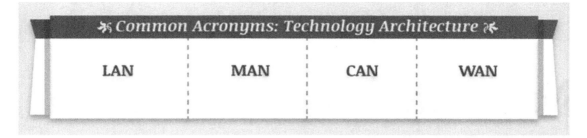

Figure 2-1. Technology Architecture Acronyms

- **Local Area Network (LAN)**: A local area network is a computer network that interconnects computers in a smaller geographic area.

- **Metropolitan Area Network (MAN)**: A Metropolitan area network is a network designed for a specific geographic locality such as a town or a city.

- **Wide Area Network (WAN)**: A wide area network covers a larger geographic area such as a regional or national boundary. The Internet is an example of a WAN.

- **Campus Area Network (CAN)**: A campus area network is a computer network that is made up of an interconnection of local area networks (LANs) within a limited geographical area.

Network Topology

Network topology describes how the network is physically arranged. There are five specific types of topology that you should be aware of—ring, bus, star, mesh, and hybrid:

- **Ring Topology**: In a ring topology, each device is directly connected to two other devices forming a closed loop. What do you suppose will happen should one of the devices fail? If you said "bring down the network," you would be correct, which is a big disadvantage of this topology.

- **Bus Topology**: Network components that are connected to the same cable, sometimes called "the bus," are arranged in the bus topology.

- **Star Topology**: With the star topology, network components are connected to a central point such as a hub or a switch. Larger networks may use more than one topology at the same time resulting in a mixed or hybrid topology.

- **Mesh Topology**: In a mesh topology, all the network components have a direct point-to-point link with every other network component.

- **Hybrid Topology**: A hybrid topology is a combination of two or more topologies. For example, a ring and a bus topology can be combined together to create a hybrid topology.

Now that you've learned how a network topology describes how a network is physically arranged, it's important to understand that you can use the same terms to describe the logical topology, the way in which data are transmitted between network nodes. To make matters a little more confusing, a network's logical topology does not necessarily match its physical topology.

Network Protocol

Network protocols are the rules and conventions used for communication. A protocol is a format for exchanging information that all agree on. Parameters include data compression method, type of error checking, and the signal when data is finished receiving or transmitting (see Figure 2-2):

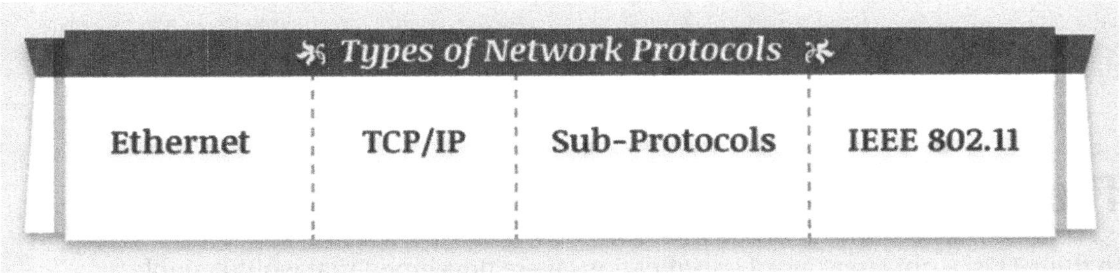

✶ Types of Network Protocols ✶			
Ethernet	TCP/IP	Sub-Protocols	IEEE 802.11

Figure 2-2. *Types of Network Protocols*

- **Ethernet**: The IEEE 802.3 standard specifies all forms of Ethernet media and interfaces. Ethernet is the most widely implemented LAN standard.

- **TCP/IP**: If you browse the Web, then you are using the Transmission Control Protocol/Internet Protocol more commonly referred to as TCP/IP. TCP/IP is a suite of specialized protocols and has become the standard because it is open; rather than proprietary, it is flexible, and it is routable.

- **Sub-protocols**: When you surf the Web, you will be using a few of the sub-protocols including dynamic host control protocol (DHCP), hypertext transfer protocol (HTTP), file transfer protocol (FTP), and domain name system (DNS). When you turned on your computer, the computer requested an IP address from the DHCP server. All devices that want to use the Internet require an IP address. After opening your browser, you type in the name of the website that you wish to visit, for example, `www.cssia.org/`. A server running the domain name system (DNS) translates the easily remembered domain names that we use into its IP address equivalent. The home page from the CSSIA site is then displayed in your browser.

- Protocols are used throughout networking to provide communication standards. The Institute of Electrical and Electronics Engineers (IEEE) is a professional association and is one of the leading networking standards organizations.

- **IEEE 802.11**: IEEE 802.11 is the standard for wireless networking. Communication protocols that define how wireless LANs operate.

The OSI Model

In the 1980s, a universal set of specifications were developed that would enable any computer platform to communicate openly. The result was the Open Systems Interconnection (OSI) model. The OSI model is useful for understanding computer-to-computer communications over a network.

The model is divided into seven layers. At each layer, protocols perform services that are unique to that layer. The protocols for that service also interact with protocols in the layers directly above and below. At the bottom, you have the Physical layer services that act on the network cables and connectors to issue and receive signals. At the top, you have the Application layer protocols that interact with the software that you use such as an email program or a web browser.

The OSI model is a theoretical representation of what happens between two nodes communicating on a network. For specific details regarding each layer and a graphic representation read "How OSI Works" (`https://electricalacademia.com/computer/osi-model-layers-functions/`).

IP Packet

In order for networks to share information and resources, rules must be followed for effective communication. A large amount of data must be broken into smaller, more manageable chunks called packets before transmission can occur from one computer to another. Each protocol has its own definition of a packet.

Figure 2-3 breaks down an IP packet into two main sections: the header and the data (also referred to as the payload). The header section contains all of the information required to describe the packet, such as where the packet is going (the IP address of the destination) or where the packet is coming from (the source IP address). Of course, the data itself is contained in the payload.

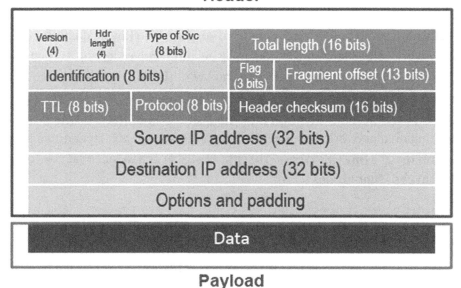

Figure 2-3. *Graphic Breakdown of an IP Packet into Two Main Sections: The Header and the Data, Also Called the Payload*

TCP vs. UDP

It is important to understand the differences between a Transmission Control Protocol (TCP) and a User Datagram Protocol (UDP). A UDP is a connectionless, unreliable protocol, while Transmission Control Protocol (TCP) is connection-oriented and ensures that packets are processed in the same order in which they were sent.

When you send a package with FedEx, you have a tracking number that you can use to make sure that the package was received by the intended party, very similar to TCP. Contrast this scenario with that of sending mail by depositing it in a mailbox. You hope that the other party receives it, but you cannot track it. You do not receive a confirmation that it arrived. This second scenario is much like UDP.

Three-Way Handshake

One of the characteristics of the TCP protocol is that it is reliable and guaranteed. Therefore, systems must follow a specific pattern when TCP is used to establish communication (see Figure 2-4).

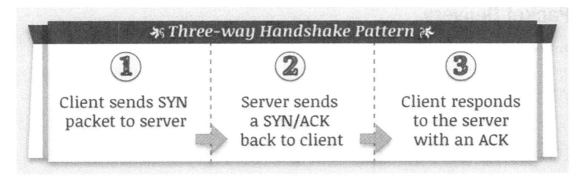

Figure 2-4. *Three-Way Handshake Pattern*

This pattern is referred to as the three-way handshake. To illustrate this pattern, let's use a phone call. You call your friend—that is the SYN. When your friend answers the phone and says "hello"—that is the SYN/ACK. When you respond, that is the ACK. Now, the conversation is ready to go forward. Because TCP is guaranteed and reliable, it is popular for many network applications and services such as HTTP, FTP, and Telnet.

Internet Control Message Protocol (ICMP)

In addition to TCP and UDP, the Internet Control Message Protocol (ICMP) is another widely used protocol. ICMP is a connectionless protocol designed to carry small messages quickly with minimal overhead. ICMP is a control and information protocol and is used by network devices to determine

- If a remote network is available

- The length of time to reach a remote network

- The best route for packets to take when traveling to another network

The ping command uses ICMP to determine whether the host on the other end of the command can be reached. Unfortunately, the ICMP protocol has also been used to execute denial-of-service (DoS) attacks because the packets are so small and can be generated by a single system in a short period of time.

15

Packet Delivery

To deliver a packet, you have to know where it is going. Packet delivery can be either local, which applies to packets being delivered on a local network, or remote, which are packets being delivered outside your local network (see Figure 2-5).

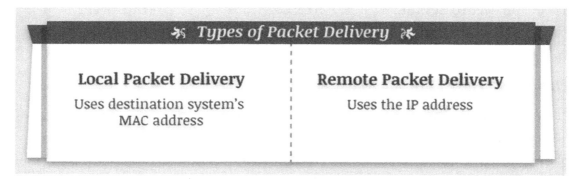

Figure 2-5. *Types of Packet Delivery*

Local Packet Delivery

Local packet delivery uses the system's hardware address or Media Access Control (MAC) address. Each network device has a unique hardware address assigned to it by the manufacturer. A MAC address is made up of six pairs of hexadecimal digits. For example, I can use the command ipconfig/all to locate the physical address of my Ethernet card which is 08:00:27:00:10:9D. The first three sets of digits are unique to a manufacturer, and the remaining three sets are unique to the card itself. Figure 2-6 provides an example of a local packet delivery process using images, directional arrows, and numbers identifying what occurs at each step.

Remote Packet Delivery

Remote packet delivery uses the IP address. IP addresses are 32-bit numbers that are usually referred to in their decimal equivalent, like 192.168.1.100. Before sending a packet, the system will first determine if the destination IP address is on a local or remote network. After determining that the packet is indeed destined for a remote network, it forwards the packet to the network gateway, the router.

Routers are used to interconnect networks, and the process of moving packets from one network to another is called routing. If a router does not know where the destination network is, it forwards the packet to its defined gateway. This process is repeated until the packet arrives at the router serving the destination network. At this point, the router will use local packet delivery to forward the packet to the appropriate MAC address of the destination system.

Domain Name System (DNS)

The domain name system (DNS) is a hierarchical naming system for any resources connected to the Internet or a private network. DNS translates the domain name, cssia. org, to its IP address, 67.179.77.158. Most of us cannot remember a bunch of IP addresses for the websites that we visit. Domain names are much easier for us to remember. Review Figure 2-6, which provides an example of a local packet delivery process using images, directional arrows, and numbers identifying what occurs at each step.

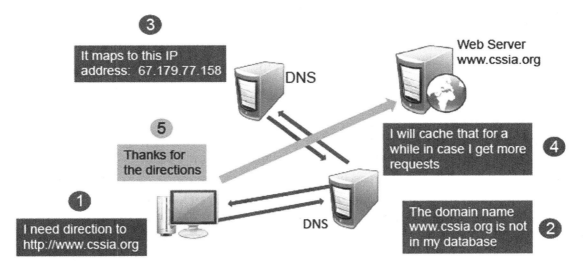

Figure 2-6. *Illustration of a Local Packet Delivery Process Including the Five Steps Used to Indicate What Occurs to Arrive at* `www.cssia.org`

Routing

Routing is the process of moving packets between networks. A router is the network device that forwards packets between networks. Routers use forwarding tables to determine where a packet goes. You may have a cable modem, a router which connects to the Internet through an Internet service provider more commonly known as an ISP. Routers look at the destination address to determine where to send the packet.

IP Addressing

As previously mentioned, IP addresses are 32-bit numbers represented as 4 groups, or octets, of 8-bits each and are commonly referred to in their decimal equivalents rather than the binary representation. Of the 32 bits, some are used for the network portion of the address, and the others are used for the host portion of the address.

Subnetting

Subnetting is used to divide the 32 bits into the network portion of the address vs. the host portion of the address. The subnet mask is used. For example, you may have an IP address of 192.168.1.100 and the subnet mask is 255.255.255.0 which is the default Class C subnet mask. Therefore, the first three octets represent the network portion of the IP address (192.168.1.0), and the last octet represents the host portion of the address. When TCP/IP is configured on a device, both an IP address and a subnet mask are required.

Classes of Network Addresses

There are three classes of network addresses as shown in the slide. With a Class A network, the number of possible networks is smaller since only the first octet is used for the network portion of the address, but a Class A network supports 16,777,214 hosts on each network. A Class C network is just the opposite. You can have more networks since a Class C uses 3 octets for the network portion of the address, but each network supports only 253 hosts.

- **Class A**: 0.0.0.0 thru 126.255.255.255

- **Class B**: 128.0.0.0 thru 191.255.255.255

- **Class C**: 192.0.0.0 thru 223.255.255.255

- **Class D**: 224.0.0.0 thru 224.0.0.0 (multicast)

- **Class E**: 240.0.0.0 thru 255.255.255.255 (reserved)

Reserved Addresses

There are a number of IP addresses that are reserved and cannot be used by any devices on your network (see Table 2-1). Each network requires a broadcast address, and the last address of a network is used for that purpose. The loopback address, 127.0.0.1, is reserved for testing the transmission.

Private IP addresses fall into three ranges. These addresses are commonly used in home, office, and corporate networks and were originally intended to delay having the IPv4 addresses run out. Private addresses are not allocated to any specific organization, and IP packets addressed by them cannot be transmitted onto the Internet.

Table 2-1. *Types of Reserved Addresses*

	Table head
Unusable addresses	Broadcast address: 10.10.10.255 Subnet network address: 10.10.10.0
Automatic private IP address	169.254.0.1 thru 169.255.255.254
Loopback address	127.0.0.1
Private addresses	.0.0.0 thru 10.255.255.255 172.16.0.0 thru 172.31.255.255 192.168.0.0 thru 192.168.255.255

Classless IP Addressing

Classless IP Addressing is used to reduce the wastage of IP addresses in a block. There is no fixed length for the network and hosts as it is fixed in the classful IP addressing. In classless IP addressing, the number of bits for network mask are defined with the IP address with a symbol "/".

Network Address Translation (NAT)

To understand network address translation (NAT), we first need to understand the difference between a private IP address which is non-routable and a public IP address which is routable (see Figure 2-7). The previous slide defined three address ranges that are used for private IP addresses. When a server using the dynamic host control protocol (DHCP) is used to automatically assign IP addresses to network nodes, private IP addresses are assigned. Because private IP addresses are non-routable, there needs to be an "interpreter" in place to substitute a routable address. Without a routable IP address, a user would be confined to his network and would not be able to surf the Web, for example. NAT is the process of modifying IP address information in the IP packet header so that the packet can be transmitted across a traffic routing device.

Many home networks use NAT, a feature found in routers, so that multiple hosts on the home network can access the Internet using a single public IP address.

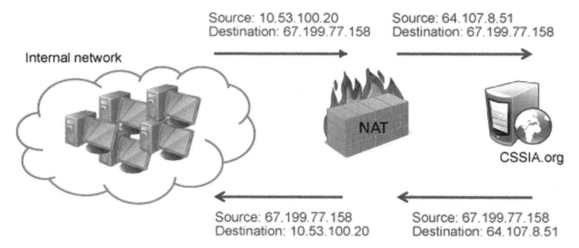

Figure 2-7. *Illustration of How NAT Is Used to Modify IP Address Information As Described in the Preceding Section*

Security Zones

Because the first aspect of security is a layered defense, different zones are designed to provide layers of defense (see Figure 2-8). For example, a company would locate its production network in a restricted zone and use controls such as a firewall to protect it. A web server or email server, on the other hand, would be located in a less controlled zone like a demilitarized zone (DMZ) since users need to access this resource from both inside and outside the organization. The Internet is located in an uncontrolled zone—a company does not have the ability to control the Internet.

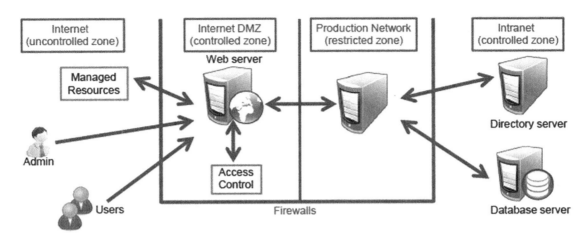

Figure 2-8. *Graphic Illustration of Security Zones Serving As a Layered Defense*

Demilitarized Zone

The demilitarized zone, or DMZ, acts as a buffer zone between unprotected areas of a network such as the Internet and protected areas like sensitive company data stores (see Figure 2-9). Traffic between these two zones can be monitored and regulated.

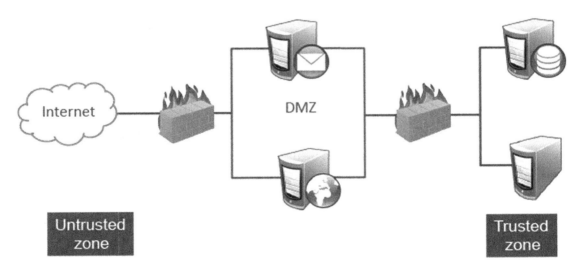

Figure 2-9. *Image Illustrates the Use of a Demilitarized Zone (DMZ) Acting as a Buffer Zone Between the Unprotected Areas, the Internet, and a Trusted Zone, Protected Company Data Stores. The DMZ Allows Traffic Between the Two Zones to be Monitored and Regulated*

Virtual LAN (VLAN)

Computers connected to different physical networks can act and communicate as if they were on the same physical network (see Figure 2-10). For example, you may have a large sales department located on a number of floors through the building. Rather than move all of the sales people on one floor, you can create a VLAN so that they can communicate and share resources. VLANs are implemented by using switches and software. Systems on separate VLANs cannot directly communicate with each other, and you can use trunking to span a single VLAN across multiple switches.

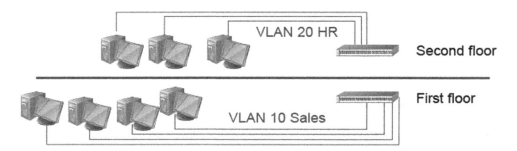

Figure 2-10. *Image Illustrates the Configuration of VLANs Connected to Different Physical Networks on the First and Second Floors of a Building to Indicate that Individuals in a Sales Department on the First Floor Can Communicate with and Share Resources Using Their Computers with Individuals in a Human Resource Department on the Second Floor*

Tunneling

Tunneling encapsulates packets so that different protocols can coexist in a single communication stream. Encryption can be used to provide confidentiality and security. Internet Protocol Security (IPsec) is an open source protocol for securing communications across any IP network such as the Internet (see Figure 2-11). If your branch office is located in a different geographic region than headquarters, you can use IPsec to tunnel your communications securely.

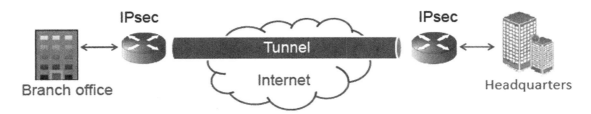

Figure 2-11. *Image Illustrates How Tunneling Encapsulates Packets so That Different Protocols Can Coexist in a Single Communication Stream As Previously Described*

Infrastructure Security: Securing a Workstation

The most common type of network device would be the workstation or the host. These devices come in many different forms, shapes, and sizes and include desktops, laptops, and tablets. These devices are normally the weakest link in most networks, so it is critical to be diligent in securing or hardening these systems. Review the following systemic safeguard recommendations for addressing common workstation vulnerabilities:

- Keep the operating system (OS) patched and up to date.

- Remove all shares that are not necessary.

- Rename the administrator account and have a strong password.

- Install an antivirus program and keep it updated.

- If no corporate firewall exists between the machine and the Internet, install a firewall.

- Use personal firewalls if the machine has an unprotected interface to the Internet.

- Turn off all services that are not needed.

- Remove methods of connecting additional devices to a workstation to copy/move data.

- Restrict physical access to the workstation to only approved personnel.

Virtualization

Virtualization technologies have become very prevalent in many organizational networks. Replacing traditional, stand-alone pairing of hardware and operating systems, today's virtualization enables us to access virtual machines, desktops, and applications on any host device anywhere on the network. This technology offers several improvements in network security but also comes with its share of potential vulnerabilities (see Figure 2-12).

Virtualization includes the ability to

- Include multiple operating systems to operate concurrently on the same hardware.

- Provide operational flexibility.

- Prevent the spread of any malware as VMs can be deleted at the end of a session.

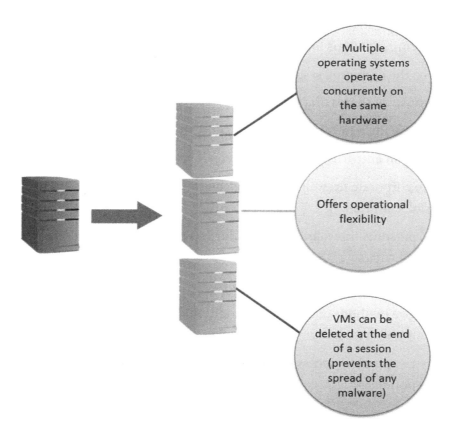

Figure 2-12. *Virtualization Vulnerabilities*

Hubs

Hubs are devices used to interconnect network workstations in the early days of networking. The use of hubs has become somewhat obsolete with the exception of special hubs placed within a network to provide greater access to multiple ports for packet sniffing. The concept of hubs is still found in many wireless access points. Virtual hubs can be created on network switches to provide the same packet-sniffing capabilities.

Hubs work to

- Connect devices in a star configuration.

- Operate at the physical layer of the OSI model.

- Create a single collision domain.

It is important to be aware that hubs are insecure. All PCs connected to a hub see all of the traffic that passes through it.

Bridges

Bridges are devices that allow us to interconnect two LAN segments or collision domains. Network switches are actually multiport bridges. Wireless access points would also be considered bridging devices (see Figure 2-13).

Bridges operate at the data link layer, filter traffic based on MAC addresses, and they reduce collisions by creating two separate collision domains. Bridges, however, have been replaced by switches.

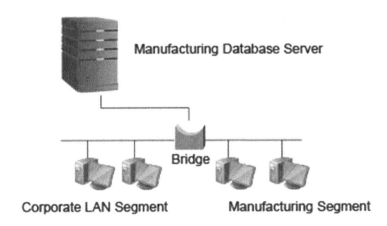

Figure 2-13. *Bridges*

Switches

Network switches are the most prevalent communications devices found in modern networks. They improve performance, segregate traffic, and provide a variety of advanced features that impact network security. They can operate at either the data link or network layers of the OSI model and can create separate collision domains for each port. A checklist for hardening network switches can be found on several places on the Web including the National CVE database, Cisco Systems' website, and NIST.

Network switches also pose their own set of vulnerabilities in the enterprise network. These vulnerabilities include

- A sniffer can only see traffic for the connected port.

- They can be attacked due to vulnerabilities in both SNMP and Telnet.

- They are subject to ARP poisoning and MAC flooding.

Routers

Routers enable us to connect one logical network to another. All corporate networks will have at least one router that is used to route traffic into and out of the organization's network referred to as the default gateway. This design has the vulnerability of being a single point of failure. As a result, many organizations choose to use two or more routers to provide multiple paths through different carriers to the Internet. Most routers have a variety of advanced security features. Routers also come with their own vulnerabilities. Like switches, there are also checklists available for hardening network routers. Here is a quick list of important key facts.

Routers

- Operate at the network layer of the OSI model.

- Connect different network segments together.

- Use routing protocols to determine optimal paths across a network.

- Form the backbone of the Internet.

- Can be attacked due to vulnerabilities in both SNMP and Telnet.

Firewalls

Most modern networks include a variety of firewalls. These devices protect the network perimeter, egress and ingress points, and the hosts on the network. Firewalls come in a variety of different forms which include stand-alone network appliances, software applications, features of operating systems, and blade or module devices that can be installed in servers or enterprise-level switches.

The function of a firewall is to control traffic coming into and out of a network. Firewalls have evolved over the years. Firewall techniques include basic packet filtering and stateful packet filtering.

Basic Packet Filtering

First-generation firewalls provided a proxy service for all network traffic. Later firewalls provided basic packet-filtering capabilities. Basic packet filtering

- Checks each packet against rules predefined on the firewall

- Is fairly simple, fast, and efficient

- Does not detect and catch all undesired packets

Stateful Packet Filtering

A variation of packet-filtering firewalls is a stateful firewall which has the ability to block all traffic entering a network unless it is traced back as a response to an outbound request. The most complex firewalls today are referred to as context-based and have the ability to do high-level packet analysis to ensure outside sources cannot hijack legitimate internally initiated sessions or communications. Stateful packet filtering

- Is a firewall that maintains the context of a conversation.

- Is more likely to detect and catch undesired packets.

- Due to overhead, network efficiency is reduced.

Modems

Modems, or modulator–demodulators, are devices that connect two network segments using different media types and communication protocols. Asynchronous modems, or phone modems, were used in the early days to connect SOHO networks to the Internet via a phone line. Synchronous modems now connect SOHO networks to the Internet via phone services (DSL), cable services, and even satellite services. Cell phones are often used today as a type of modem making the connection to the Internet through the cell phone network. Modems have several security features including MAC filtering and encryption.

Cable Modems

- Uses shared cable line.

- Other people can sniff traffic between the user and the ISP.

- Most cable modems today also implement the Data Over Cable Service Interface Specification (DOCSIS).

DSL Modems

- Uses dedicated cabling.

- Traffic cannot be sniffed between the user and the ISP.

Virtual Private Networks

Virtual private networks (VPNs) are the most common type of technology used today to establish secure communications.

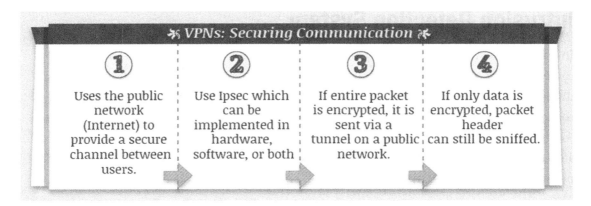

Figure 2-14. *VPNs: Securing Communication*

1. VPNs are commonly used to provide a secure communication pipe across the Internet. This is accomplished by enabling the two devices to use the same encryption algorithm and keys. All traffic sent between the two devices is encrypted and therefore secure.

2. VPN devices can be implemented in many different forms including network appliances, features within routers, and features of host operating systems.

3. VPNs can be placed at the endpoints of the network so that traffic going from one network to another is securely known as tunnel mode or secure communications can be established from one device on a network to another device on a different network or transport mode.

4. VPNs provide a high level of security; however, they pose a completely new set of vulnerabilities. When transport mode traffic is allowed to leave and enter a network, the same encryption that is protecting the data from being viewed on the Internet can prevent administrators from detecting unauthorized sensitive information entering or leaving their own network.

Intrusion Detection System

Intrusion detection systems (IDS) and intrusion prevention systems (IPS) are designed to detect signs of attacks or unusual traffic on a network. IDS and IPS systems come in different forms including network appliances, modules within network switches and routers, and as an advanced feature on network devices and different operating systems. An intrusion detection system will send an alert when it detects patterns such as a signature indicating an attack or unusual traffic also known as an anomaly. IPS systems not only generate an alert, but they can take corrective actions as well.

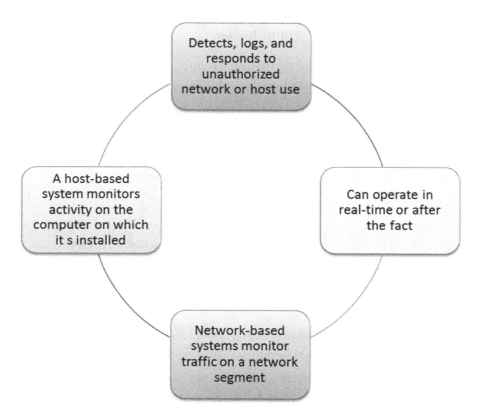

Figure 2-15. *Intrusion Detection System*

Mobile Devices

One of the most common vulnerabilities on today's networks is mobile devices. These devices include laptops, tablets, smartphones, and other wireless devices such as cameras. These devices can infect other devices on the network, be used to capture sensitive data, or launch internal attacks on other host or network devices. It is important to keep in mind that a mobile device

- Can act as transmission vectors for viruses

- Can be used to remove sensitive material off-site

- Can be used as part of a Bluetooth attack

Media Cables

There are several types of media cables that have different uses and applications. Please read Types of Media for details on the following cable types: coaxial, UTP/STP, fiber, unguided media–infrared (IR), and unguided media–(RF)/microwave.

Security Concerns for Transmission Media

Network media pose several different types of vulnerabilities. These vulnerabilities include disconnection, packet sniffing, and unauthorized access to rogue devices. It is important to address physical security concerns. Network connections should be labeled and monitored in order to control unauthorized access. All unused media ports should be disabled.

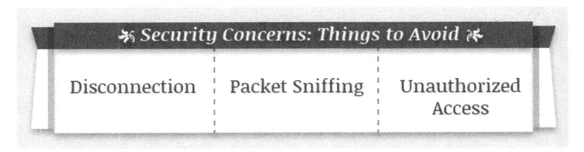

Figure 2-16. Security Concerns: Things to Avoid

- **Disconnection**: Access to a server by an unauthorized individual

- **Packet Sniffing**: Access to switches and routers by an unauthorized individual.

- **Unauthorized Access**: Access to network connections by an unauthorized individual

Object Reuse

Storage media poses greater challenges and risk in modern networks. Today's media can store far more data and be written to and read from much faster. All storage media that contains sensitive data should be controlled, monitored, and encrypted when possible. These devices should also be properly managed when they are decommissioned and no longer used.

Network-Attached Storage

Most modern networks now include mass storage devices which include NAS (network-attached storage), SAN (storage area network), and iSCSI. These technologies are devices that contain multiple hard drives and are used to store and share data with multiple devices on the network. Mass storage devices require high-speed connections, access control, and, in some cases, encryption technology.

SAN

- Provides only block-based storage

- Appears to the client OS as a disk visible in disk management

NAS

- Provides both storage and a file system

- Appears to the client OS as a file server (client can map drives)

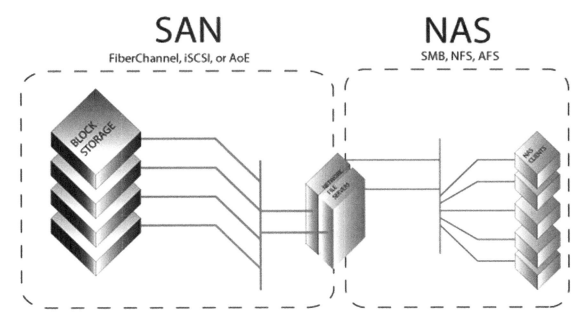

Figure 2-17. *Storage Area Network (SAN) and Network-Attached Storage (NAS)*

Summary

It is important to have an understanding of network fundamentals needed to build network security. Be familiar with the basic network architectures and protocols which will help you to implement secure network administration principles. It will be important to use common protocols discussed in this lesson as needed to employ infrastructure security. Keep in mind the importance of what you learned about routing, and address translation which will help you further understand the vulnerabilities and threats that can be exploited.

Resources

- **Local Area Network**: www.webopedia.com/TERM/L/local_area_ network_LAN.html

- **Metropolitan Area Network**: www.webopedia.com/TERM/M/MAN.html

- **Wide Area Network**: www.comptia.org/content/guides/what-is-a-wide-area-network

- **Campus Area Network**: www.webopedia.com/TERM/C/CAN.html

- **OSI Layers Working**: https://electricalacademia.com/computer/osi-model-layers-functions/

CHAPTER 3

Wireless and Intrusion Detection System Network Security

An intrusion detection system (IDS) is a key technology in protecting our network and information systems. This technology is now found in most networks. Anyone entering the information security field should be familiar with its operation and implementation. A variation of the IDS is the intrusion prevention system (IPS). In this lesson you will learn about various firewall technologies, honeypots, and honeynets.

By the end of this lesson, you will be able to

1. Explain the security function and purpose of network devices and technologies.

2. Apply and implement secure network administration principles.

3. Implement a wireless network in a secure manner.

Introduction to Wireless Networking

Wireless networking transmits packets using radio waves rather than a physical cable. With the popularity of wireless networking came the attempts to breach the security of these transmissions. Wireless security is a very important topic since more devices are being designed to use wireless to send data.

Wireless is a concern from a security standpoint because there is no control over the physical layer—it is not wired. We will take a look at the different wireless systems in use today. The Wireless Application Protocol (WAP) was the initial attempt to handle

© Ahmed F. Sheikh 2020
A. F Sheikh, *CompTIA Security+ Certification Study Guide*, https://doi.org/10.1007/978-1-4842-6234-4_3

the demand for additional wireless data services. We will take a look at how wireless has evolved and what security measures can be adopted.

The IEEE 802.11 protocol is the set of standards for implementing a wireless local area network. Think of the devices that you may have that are wireless: a phone, a tablet, a headset, or a mouse and keyboard just to name a few. Bluetooth is a wireless technology standard for exchanging data over short distances and are used to create what are known as personal area networks (PANs).

Think About It

- Wireless networking is the transmission of packetized data by means of a physical topology that does not use direct physical links.

- IEEE 802.11 is a family of protocols that have been standardized by the IEEE for wireless local area networks (LANs).

- Wireless Application Protocol (WAP) was one of the pioneers of mobile data applications.

- Bluetooth is a short-range wireless protocol typically used on small devices such as mobile phones.

802.11

The 802.11 protocol is made up of several different specifications. Each operates at a different frequency and speed. If you were to go and purchase a new laptop, you would want to make sure that it uses the latest wireless standard. Please review the specifications chart (Table 3-1) for details on speed and frequency range.

Table 3-1. *Chart for Details on Speed and Frequency Range*

Specification	Speed	Frequency range
802.11a	54 Mbps	5.2 GHz
802.11b	11 Mbps	2.4 GHz
802.11g	11 Mbps/54 Mbps	2.4 GHz
802.11i	11 Mbps/54 Mbps	2.4 GHz
802.11n	124–248 Mbps	2.4 GHz/5.2 GHz

WAP

As previously mentioned, WAP is a protocol for accessing information over a wireless network. As the mobile networks' capabilities increase, though, carriers are adopting a more IP-centric routing methodology. WAP gap involves confidentiality of information where the two different networks meet, the WAP gateway. It is important to be aware of the following:

1. Wireless Transport Layer Security (WTLS) is a lightweight security protocol designed for WAP.

2. WTLS acts as the security protocol for the WAP network; TLS protocol, formerly known as Secure Sockets Layer (SSL), to ensure confidentiality. TLS is the standard for the Internet—the WAP gateway performs translation from one encryption standard to the other. There are several known security vulnerabilities.

3. WTLS implements integrity through the use of message authentication codes (MACs).

WAP Vulnerabilities

A WAP gateway translates the encryption standards used by the wireless network and WTLS and the Internet which uses TLS. There is some concern at this point where the two different networks meet. The translation means that all messages seen by the WAP gateway are in plaintext. Threats to the WAP gateway can be handled by careful infrastructure design. Keep in mind that there are key vulnerabilities associated with a WAP:

- WTLS acts as the security protocol for the WAP network; TLS is the standard for the Internet—the WAP gateway performs translation from one encryption standard to the other.

- A WAP can face disruptions or attacks because it aggregates at well-known points: the cellular antenna towers.

- WAP gap involves confidentiality of information where the two different networks meet, the WAP gateway.

Bluetooth

Bluetooth is a short-range, low-power protocol. As previously mentioned, Bluetooth transmits data in a personal area network, or PAN, and can include devices such as mobile phones, laptops and printers. Bluetooth has gone through several version releases. Easy configuration is a characteristic of Bluetooth, so there is no need for network addresses. Bluetooth uses pairing to establish the relationship between devices. When establishing the pairing, a passkey is entered into both devices.

Bluetooth vulnerabilities have surfaced, but due to the limited range of Bluetooth, the victim and the attack need to be within range of each other.

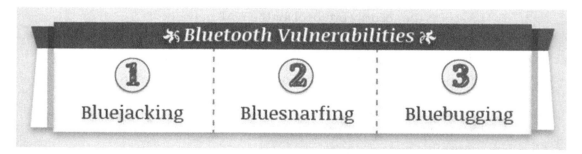

Figure 3-1. *Bluetooth Vulnerabilities*

1. **Bluejacking** is the term used for sending unauthorized messages to another Bluetooth device. A variation of this is to send a shocking image to the other device.

2. **Bluesnarfing** occurs when the attacker copies the victim's information from his device. This information can include emails and contact lists.

3. **Bluebugging** occurs when the attacker uses Bluetooth to establish a serial connection to a device which allows full control over that device.

To improve security, Bluetooth should always have discoverable mode turned off unless you are actively trying to pair your device.

Consider the Following Important Bluetooth Feature Information:

- A short-range (approx. 32 feet), low-power wireless protocol transmitting in the 2.4 GHz band.

- Transmits data in personal area networks (PANs) through mobile phones, laptops, printers, etc.

- Version 1.2 allows speeds up to 721 Kbps and improves resistance to interference.

- Bluetooth 2.0 introduced enhanced data rate (EDR), which allows the transmission of up to 3.0 Mbps.

802.11 Modulation

In telecommunications, frequency modulation conveys information over a carrier wave by varying its frequency. Spread-spectrum techniques transmit on a bandwidth which is larger than the original frequency:

- **Direct-sequence spread spectrum (DSSS)** is a modulation type that spreads the traffic sent over the entire bandwidth.

- **Orthogonal frequency division multiplexing (OFDM)** separates the data to be transmitted into smaller chunks and then transmits the chunks on several sub-channels.

DSSS and OFDM are techniques that are used to avoid interference. Please review Table 3-2 for details regarding protocols and modulations.

Table 3-2. *Chart for Details Regarding Protocols and Modulations*

802.11 Protocol	Modulation
a	OFDM
b	DSSS
g	OFDM
n	OFDM
y	OFDM

802.11 Individual Standards

Each individual standard can differ in speed and frequency. While wireless transmissions can penetrate walls or other objects, performance is best when both the access point and network client have an unobstructed view of each other. It should be pointed out that the 2.4-GHz bank is used by many common household devices such as cordless phones, baby monitors, and microwave ovens. See Table 3-3.

Table 3-3. *Various Standards and Their Speed and Frequency*

Protocol	Speed and frequency
802.11a	• Supports traffic on the 5-GHz band, allowing speeds up to 54 Mbps
802.11b	• Provides for multiple-rate Ethernet over 2.4-GHz spread-spectrum wireless • Transfer rates of 1 Mbps, 2 Mbps, 5.5 Mbps, and 11 Mbps
802.11g	• Allows the faster speeds of the 5-GHz specification on the 2.4-GHz band
802.11n	• Offers speeds up to 248 Mbps

802.11 Protocol

Authentication is handled by having clients perform a handshake when attempting to associate to the access point (AP). Association is required before the access point will allow the client to use the AP to access the network. One of the parameters needed in the handshake is the service set identifier (SSID).

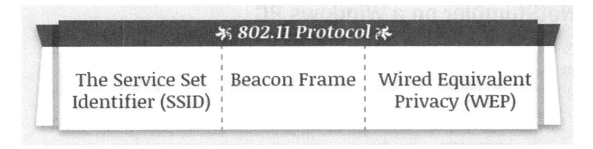

Figure 3-2. *802.11 Protocol*

SSID is a name that ensures that you are connecting to the correct AP. The service set identifier (SSID) setting should limit access only to the authorized users of the wireless network.

Beacon frame is an 802.11 management frame for the network and contains several different fields, such as the timestamp and beacon interval but most importantly the SSID.

Wired equivalent privacy, or WEP, was the first attempt at maintaining confidentiality on wireless networks. WEP uses the RC4 stream cipher to encrypt the data as it is transmitted through the air. Unfortunately, WEP has an inherent problem which makes it extremely easy to exploit.

Attacking 802.11

Wireless is a popular target. An attacker can probe a building for wireless access from the street without giving any indication that an attempted intrusion is taking place. Most APs do not have an alert that occurs when a user is associating with it. Another reason that wireless attacks are popular is the low cost of the equipment needed.

To find a wireless network, you can go war-driving. War-drivers drive around with a wireless located program and record the networks found at various locations. Variations of this term are war-dialing (dialing a list of phone numbers looking for modem-connected computers), war-walking, and war-flying. The most common tools for an attacker to use are reception-based programs that listen to beacon frames and programs that promiscuously capture all traffic. A quick reference list was created to help you become familiar with the key terms associated with 802.11 attacks.

NetStumbler on a Windows PC

NetStumbler is a tool that helps to detect Wireless LANs. This program is used to verify network configurations, finding areas of poor WLAN coverage, and detecting causes of wireless interference. An attacker might use this tool to listen to the beacon frames output by access points to capture the information.

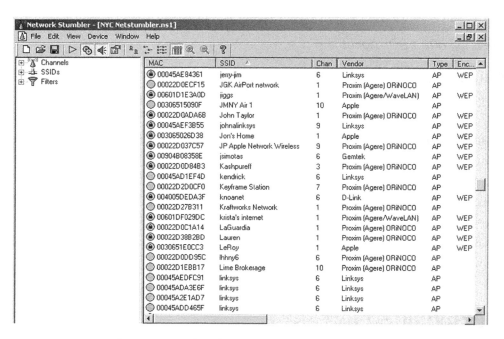

Figure 3-3. *An Attacker Listens for the Beacon Frames of APs That Are Within Range of the Card Attached to the NetStumbler Computer, Logging All Available Information*

Windows Displaying Access Points

For those that have used a laptop to connect to a wireless network, you may have seen the window displayed by a Microsoft operating system that lists the wireless networks that are active in the area. You can choose the one that you want to connect to.

Figure 3-4. *Screenshot: Windows Displays a List of SSIDs Active in the Area and Prompts the User to Choose One to Connect to*

New Security Protocols

Since WEP was shown to be vulnerable, new security protocols have come along. WPA2 provides stronger data protection and network access control for both enterprises (WPA2-Enterprise) and consumers (WPA2-Personal). WPA2 uses the AES encryption algorithm and 802.1 x authentications.

WPA2-Personal utilizes a passphrase, while WPA2-Enterprise verifies network users through a server.

Consider the Following Important New Security Protocol Information:

- Wi-Fi Protected Access (WPA and WPA2) uses 802.1X to provide authentication and uses Advanced Encryption Standard (AES) as the encryption protocol.

- Temporal Key Integrity Protocol (TKIP) overcomes the Wired Equivalency Protocol (WEP) key weakness, as a key is used on only one packet.

- 802.1X protocol supports a wide variety of authentication methods and fits into existing authentication systems such as a Remote Authentication Dial-In User Service (RADIUS) and Lightweight Directory Access Protocol (LDAP).

Implementing 802.X

Three common methods are used to implement 802.1x: EAP–TLS, EAP–TTLS, and EAP–MD5. EAP stands for Extensible Authentication Protocol. The client that wants to be authenticated is called the supplicant. The server doing the authentication is called the authentication server. The wireless access point is called the authenticator. With 802.1x, the authenticator can be simple which is ideal for a wireless access point since it is usually small and has little memory or processing power.

Three common methods for implementing 802.1X

1. **EAP–TLS** relies on TLS, an attempt to standardize the SSL structure to pass credentials.

2. **EAP–Tunneled TLS Protocol (EAP–TTLS)** allows the use of legacy authentication protocols (PAP, CHAP MS–CHAP, or MS–CHAP-V2).

3. **EAP–MD5** improves the authentication of the client to the AP but not the security of your AP.

Note   Use encryption with WPA or WPA2, and turn off SSID broadcasting to help avoid some scanning.

Types of Intrusion Detection Systems

An intrusion detection system (IDS) can be implemented in a variety of different forms from a stand-alone appliance to a feature built into the operating system of a switch or a router. They can also be host-based as an application or a feature of an operating system or database. When categorizing an IDS, we typically identify two types: host-based and network-based. The host-based systems examine signatures and anomalies on the native host to identify potential attacks or unusual activity. A network-based IDS resides on border routers or appliances and identifies unusual network traffic or signatures of a network-based attack.

Review the following types of intrusion detection systems:

- **Host-Based IDS (HIDS)** examines activity on an individual system.

- **Network-based IDS (NIDS)** examines activity on the network.

- **Signature-based IDS** relies heavily on a predefined set of attack and traffic patterns called signatures.

- **Anomaly-based (heuristic) IDS** monitors activity and attempts to classify it as either "normal" or "anomalous."

IDS Components

Although IDS systems come in a variety of forms, all IDS systems have several common components. The core elements consist of a traffic/data collector and an analytic engine. These elements require external components in order to perform analytics. These external components consist of a signature database, critical files, and, of course, the network traffic to be analyzed. The device is configured and controlled through a user interface. IDS systems use these components to generate log files and alarm messages. This information can be compiled into a report that can be delivered to the user interface, a syslog server, or directly to an administrator via email or a text message.

It is important to detail the following roles:

- A **traffic collector/sensor** collects activity/events for the IDS to examine.

- An **analysis engine** examines the collected network traffic and compares it to known patterns of suspicious activity.

- A **signature database** is a collection of patterns and definitions of known suspicious activity.

- A **user interface** provides alerts and the means to interact and operate the IDS.

Review Figure 3-5 for an example of how these roles are applied.

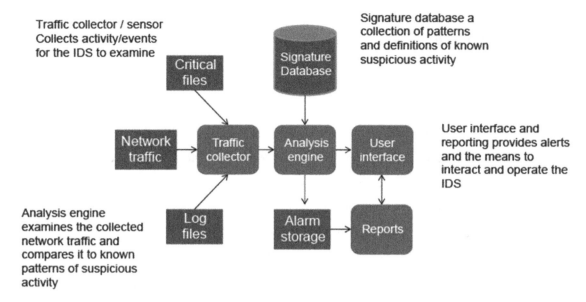

Figure 3-5. *IDS Components: This Graphic Illustrates How the Traffic Controller, Analysis Engine, Signature Database, and User Interface Function Within an IDS System*

NIDS Placement

The placement of IDS systems is critical to their effectiveness and their ability to interpret intrusions. IDS systems can be placed on the outside of a firewall as early warning systems in the DMZ or in the private network. IDS systems can also reside on any host within the network. Typically, host-based IDS reside on the most critical systems including database servers, critical application servers, and network administration systems:

- Placed before the firewall, the NIDS will see all traffic coming in from the Internet, including the traffic that the firewall stops.

- NIDS sensor generates a large number of alarms.

- Placed after the firewall, the NIDS sensor sees and analyzes traffic passed into the corporate network results in fewer alarms.

Network IDS

It is important to review the advantages and disadvantages associated with a network IDS system in place. IDS systems are very effective in identifying common types of network attacks, are fairly inexpensive to purchase and implement, and can make the task of intrusion detection and prevention automated and continuous. Disadvantages of IDS include the expertise necessary to interpret logs, alarms, and reports. They are also ineffective in analyzing encrypted traffic. They can be bypassed if an attacker knows that an IDS is in place. A network IDS is ineffectual at identifying host-based attacks.

Advantages

- Providing IDS coverage requires fewer systems.

- Deployment, maintenance, and upgrade costs are usually lower.

- Visibility into all network traffic and correlates attacks among multiple systems.

Disadvantages

- Ineffective when traffic is encrypted

- Cannot see traffic that does not cross it

- Must be able to handle high volumes of traffic

- Does not know about activity on the hosts themselves

Active vs. Passive NIDS

The difference between an IDS and an IPS is that IDS systems are passive. They generate alarms, log entries, and reports but have limited capabilities to respond to an intrusion. IPS systems are active and can be programmed and "taught" to take actions based on specific types of signatures and anomalies. These actions can include shutting down ports, closing TCP/IP connections, and blocking traffic from specific locations. They can also be taught to collect data that is being accessed by an unauthorized agent.

Passive NIDS: A passive NIDS generates an alarm when it matches a pattern and does not interact with the traffic in any way.

Active NIDS: Reactive response to an attack such as a TCP reset.

TCP Reset: The TCP reset is the most common defensive ability for an active NIDS. The reset message (RST) tells both sides of the connection to drop the session and stop communicating immediately.

Signatures

IDS signatures are typically categorized into two groups: content-based signatures and context-based signatures.

Content-based signatures

- They look for specific characters or strings.

- They are normally the simplest type of signatures to build.

- Easy to build and look for simple things, such as a certain string of characters or a certain flag set in a TCP packet.

Context-based signatures

- They look for matching patterns of activity.

- They are generally more complex and require more storage and processing capabilities.

IDS Matrix

An IDS can be effective; however, operators need to understand that an IDS is not foolproof. Two of the more common issues are false-positive and false-negative alarms. The false-positive is when an IDS identifies normal or authorized events as intrusions. It takes an experienced specialist to identify these issues. A false-negative, on the other hand, is when the IDS does not detect an intrusion. In many cases, an IDS can be trained to identify traffic it sees as authorized to still generate an alarm. True-positives occur when an actual intrusion is detected. A true-negative occurs when an IDS does not generate an alarm for authorized conditions. Machine learning and artificial intelligence can be used to train the IDS in order to minimize the false-positive and false-negative alarms.

Table 3-4. *Common Issues in IDS*

	True	False
Positive	True-positive An alarm WAS generated, and a present condition should be alarmed	False-positive An alarm WAS generated, and there is no present condition which should be alarmed
Negative	True-negative An alarm was NOT generated, and there is not present condition which should be alarmed	False-negative An alarm was NOT generated, and a present condition should be alarmed

IDS Detection Models

An IDS can be trained to identify anomalies and system misuse. Two types of detection models include anomaly detection model and the misuse detection model.

Anomaly Detection Model: The anomaly detection model is based on the ability to identify variances from normal network and host behavior. An example is a high utilization of bandwidth on a specific port during off hours. Another common anomaly is an unusual amount of traffic leaving or entering a host that handles sensitive information. The anomaly detection model can also detect what it perceives as unauthorized, encrypted data traversing the network or being sent or received by a host on the network.

Misuse Detection Model: The misuse detection model detects suspicious activity that violates the organization's policies. The misuse detection model is less complex and more efficient than anomaly detection. An example of misuse detection is the unauthorized use of a VPN. This model can also detect events like access during unauthorized times, hijacking or the use of covert channels, or password cracking.

Firewall

Firewalls have become part of standard operations in most organizations. Firewalls can be hardware- or software-based or a combination of the two. A firewall is designed to examine traffic and then allow or block that traffic based on the organization's policies.

A firewall operates using a multitude of different processes which include proxy services, access control lists, network address translation, basic packet filtering, stateful packet filtering, and context-based packet filtering.

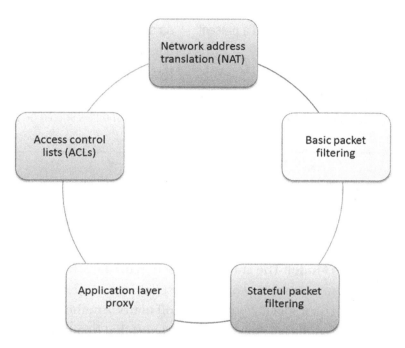

Figure 3-6. *Firewall: The Graphic Provides Details of Five Aspects of a Firewall to Help You Understand How It Works*

Network address translation (NAT) is the process of translating inside private IP addresses to a public IP address. NAT also handles the reverse process—getting the inbound traffic to the appropriate inside host private IP address. NAT provides two major benefits. First, it protects the inside hosts' addresses from outside attackers. Secondly, it expands potential addressing pools by using reserved, private addresses.

Basic packet filtering is the ability to allow or block packets based on content. The content can include addresses, ports, or combinations.

Stateful packet filtering blocks all inbound traffic except traffic that is in response to an outbound request. This allows our internal network users to access outside resources while at the same time blocking all unauthorized access to the inbound network. Context-based packet filtering is the most complex and requires greater storage and processing capabilities. It actually interrogates traffic to ensure that an outside attacker cannot hijack stateful authorized inbound traffic.

Proxy services use one device to handle all inbound and outbound traffic. This process prevents any individual host from directly communicating to the outside network. Proxy servers have an inherent vulnerability—they pose a single point of failure and also a bottleneck point on the network.

Access control lists, or ACLs, are a group of rules that specify which traffic can be allowed or blocked by the firewall. These rules are typically based on source and destination addresses or source and destination ports.

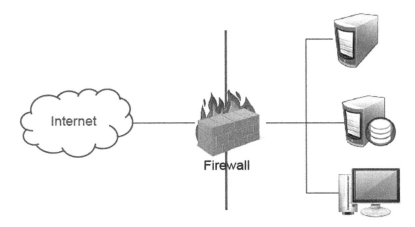

Figure 3-7. *How a Firewall Works: Graphic Illustrates How a Firewall Is Designed to Examine Traffic and Then Allow or Block Traffic Based on the Organization's Policies*

Intrusion Prevention Systems

Intrusion prevention systems can be configured to control router operations, switch operations, firewall operations, VPN establishment, and wireless access. Based on detection of signatures and anomalies, an IPS can take corrective action to stop an intrusion or attack. A warning IPS is also vulnerable to false-positives, so operator knowledge and the ability to identify a false-positive are critical in preventing an IPS from arbitrarily denying authorized activity.

Consider the Following Information About Intrusion Prevention Systems:

- They have the capability of stopping or preventing malicious attack.

- They must sit inline on the network.

- They cannot inspect encrypted traffic—some vendors include the ability to inspect SSL sessions.

- They are rated by the amount of traffic that can be processed without dropping packets.

Proxy Servers

Proxy servers provide a single point for all traffic to leave and enter the network. Proxy servers are workstations or hosts that take requests and forward them out of the network on behalf of the host. Proxy servers hide the identity of workstations within a network. They can also be used to filter or block undesirable traffic or traffic coming from an unknown, hostile threat. Proxy servers have lost what was once a high level of utilization due to their vulnerabilities which include a single point of failure and a choke point into and out of the network.

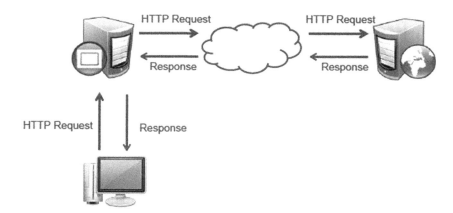

Figure 3-8. *Proxy Servers Take Client Requests and Forward to the Destination Server on Behalf of the Client and Act As a Security Application for Filtering Undesirable Traffic and for Blocking Potentially Hostile Threats*

Types of Proxy Servers

The proxy server process has been incorporated into a variety of network services including anonymizing, caching, content filtering, open proxy, reverse proxy, and web proxy.

The following list consists of basic definitions of services:

- **Anonymizing**: hides information about the requesting system when a webpage request is made

- **Caching**: Keeps local copies of popular client requests to reduce bandwidth usage and increase performance

- **Content Filtering**: Filters client requests based on acceptable use policy

- **Open Proxy**: Open for use to any Internet user and can also function in some case to anonymize requests

- **Reverse Proxy**: Sits in front of web servers to perform tasks such as filtering, shaping, or balancing incoming requests or serving up static content

- **Web Proxy**: Similar to content-filtering proxy but does not require client systems to be configured to intercept client requests

Protocol Analyzers

Protocol analyzers or signature analyzers are devices that can collect and analyze network traffic. They are used to identify performance problems, detect misconfigurations, identify misbehaving applications, establish baseline and normal traffic patterns, and debug communication problems. Protocol analyzers require that the host machine's NIC is configured to operate in promiscuous mode which means that the network card picks up traffic intended for that host and all of the other hosts on that network.

Honeypots and Honeynets

Many organizations have deployed honeypots and honeynets as early warning systems against potential attacks. Both of these systems are placed on the network and entice potential attackers to target it as easy victims within the organization. These devices may purposefully be configured with known vulnerabilities and weak security. The devices are designed to send alarms and messages that have been attacked or breached. This enables network administrators to identify the source of an attack and close the gates to prevent the attack from spreading to critical devices and systems within the organization's private network.

Host-Based IDS (HIDS)

A host-based IDS can reside on any workstation, server or host on the network. A HIDS looks to a specific host rather than monitoring all the activity on a network. Although an HIDS can be installed on any host, they are typically configured on a system storing sensitive data or providing critical services. A host-based IDS is centrally managed and monitored.

HIDs Advantages vs. Disadvantages

An HIDS can examine data after it has been received and decrypted. These systems can be very application- and operating system-specific and can be customized based on the organization's policies. Some of the disadvantages of HIDSs are that they generate a lot of log data that must be reviewed, they require expertise to interpret the logs, and they can consume resources on the local host.

Advantages

- Can be very operating system-specific

- Can reduce false-positive rates

- Can examine data after it has been decrypted

- Can be very application-specific

- Can determine how an alarm will impact a system

Disadvantages

- Must process information on every system you want to watch

- May have a high cost of ownership and maintenance

- Uses local system resources

- A focused view and cannot relate to activity around it

- If logged locally, could be compromised or disabled

Modern HIDS

All modern host-based IDSs have common components including malware detection and prevention, integrated firewall, behavioral- and signature-based IDS, application control, and enterprise management.

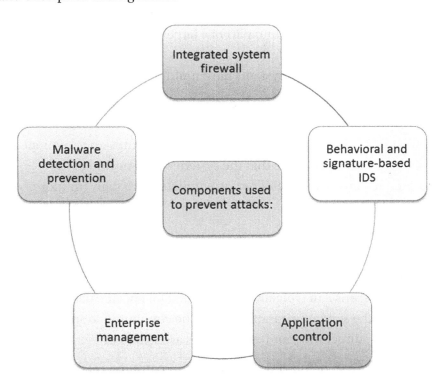

Figure 3-9. *The graphic Includes a Circle Comprising the Components That All Modern Host-Based IDSs Have in Common: Integrated System Firewall, Behavioral- and Signature-Based IDS, Application Control, Enterprise Management, Malware Detection and Prevention, and Integrated System Firewall*

Antivirus Products

All modern workstations and hosts require antivirus protection. Antivirus solutions are typically installed on individual systems (desktops and servers), but network-based antivirus capabilities are also available in many commercial gateway products. These gateway products often combine firewall, IDS/IPS, and antivirus capabilities into a single integrated platform. Most organizations also employ antivirus solutions on email servers, as email continues to be a very popular propagation method for viruses.

While the installation of a good antivirus product is still considered a necessary best practice, there is growing concern about the effectiveness of antivirus products against developing threats. Early viruses often exhibited destructive behaviors; were poorly written, modified files; and were less concerned with hiding their presence than they were with propagation. We are seeing an emergence of viruses and malware created by professionals, sometimes financed by criminal organizations that go to great lengths to hide their presence. These viruses and malware are often used to steal sensitive information or turn the infected PC into part of a larger botnet for use in spamming or attack operations.

Most enterprise-level antivirus systems have multiple features, including

- **Automated Updates**: Perhaps the most important feature of a good antivirus solution is its ability to keep itself up to date by automatically downloading the latest virus signatures on a frequent basis. This usually requires that the system be connected to the Internet in some fashion and perform updates on a daily (or more frequent) basis.

- **Automated Scanning**: Most antivirus products allow for the scheduling of automated scans, enabling the antivirus product to routinely examine the local system for infected files. These automated scans can typically be scheduled for specific days and times, and the scanning parameters can be configured to specify what drives, directories, and types of files are scanned.

- **Media Scanning**: Removable media is still a common method for virus and malware propagation, and most antivirus products can be configured to automatically scan CDs, USB drives, memory sticks, or any other types of removable media as soon as they are connected to or accessed by the local system.

- **Manual Scanning**: Many antivirus products allow the user to scan drives, files, or directories "on demand."

- **Email Scanning**: Email is still a major method of virus and malware propagation. Many antivirus products give users the ability to scan both incoming and outgoing messages as well as any attachments.

- **Resolution**: When the antivirus product detects an infected file or application, it can typically perform one of several actions. The antivirus product may quarantine the file, making it inaccessible; it may try to repair the file by removing the infection or offending code; or it may delete the infected file. Most antivirus products allow the user to specify the desired action, and some allow for an escalation in actions, such as cleaning the infected file if possible or quarantining the file if it cannot be cleaned.

Antivirus Products: Signature-Based and Heuristic Scanning

Two antivirus scanning approaches include signature-based scanning and heuristic scanning.

Signature-Based Scanning

Much like an IDS, the antivirus products scan programs, files, macros, emails, and other data for known worms, viruses, and malware. The antivirus product contains a virus dictionary with thousands of known virus signatures that must be frequently updated, as new viruses are discovered daily. This approach will catch known viruses but is limited by the virus dictionary—what it does not know about it cannot catch.

Heuristic scanning (or analysis) does not rely on a virus dictionary. Instead, it looks for suspicious behavior—anything that does not fit into a "normal" pattern of behavior for the operating system and applications running on the system being protected.

Heuristic Scanning

Heuristic scanning is a method of detecting potentially malicious or "viruslike" behavior by examining what a program or section of code does. Anything that is "suspicious" or potentially "malicious" is closely examined to determine whether or not it is a threat to the system. Using heuristic scanning, an antivirus product attempts to identify new viruses or heavily modified versions of existing viruses before they can damage your system.

Heuristic scanning typically looks for commands or instructions that are not normally found in application programs, such as attempts to access a reserved memory register. Most antivirus products use either a weight-based or rule-based system in their heuristic scanning (more effective products use a combination of both techniques). A weight-based system rates every suspicious behavior based on the degree of threat associated with that behavior. If the set threshold is passed based on a single behavior or combination of behaviors, the antivirus product will treat the process, application, macro, and so on, performing those behaviors as a threat to the system. A rules-based system compares activity to a set of rules meant to detect and identify malicious software. If part of the software matches a rule or a process, application, macro, and so on and performs a behavior that matches a rule, the antivirus software will treat that as a threat to the local system.

Personal Software Firewalls

A personal software firewall is a standard feature integrated into the operating system software. This type of firewall can be enabled or disabled and provides configuration options to permit specific types of traffic. A personal software firewall can still be used and is recommended even if a hardware-based firewall is in place on the network.

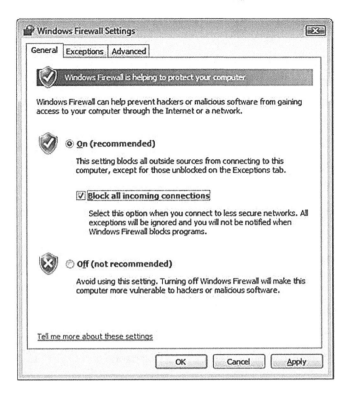

Figure 3-10. *Screenshot of Windows Firewall Settings: A Host-Based Protective Mechanism Controls Traffic Going Into and Out of a Single System*

Pop-Up Blockers and Windows Defender

In addition to firewalls, most workstations also implement pop-up blockers which prevent web content from opening new tabs or windows in the browser. These hosts also typically include security enhancement applications like Windows Defender. This software is designed for a specific operating system and can scan for spyware and potential changes to system configurations that can result in vulnerabilities and potential attacks. Windows Defender includes spyware detection and removal, scheduled scanning, automatic updates, real-time protection, software explorer, and configurable responses.

Anti-spam

With the increase of email-based attacks, anti-spam software is an essential component in protecting users on a network. Anti-spam software typically includes features like blacklists, header or subject line filtering, content filtering, trapping, custom filtering, language filtering, egress filtering, and enforcement of specific protocol control policies. Anti-spam software can reside on the email server or on email clients. Server-based solutions have become more popular because they can be centrally managed.

Anti-spam software features include

- **Blacklisting**: Rejects any mail coming from servers or domains on the blacklist

- **Header Filtering**: Looks at the message headers to see if they are forged

- **Content Filtering**: Examines message for keywords or phrases common to spam

- **Language Filtering**: Filters out emails written in certain languages

- **Trapping**: Monitors unpublished email addresses

- **Egress Filtering**: Scans mail as it leaves an organization

- **Enforcing the Specifications of the Protocol**: Enforces the technical requirements of SMTP and rejects some spam as delivery is attempted

Summary

In this lesson you had an opportunity to gain an understanding about intrusion detection systems (IDS) and how they play a key role in protecting network and information systems. You also reviewed firewall technologies, honeypots, honeynets, and the process of implementing secure administration principles and a wireless network.

CHAPTER 4

Role of People in Security—Operational and Organizational Security

In this chapter you will learn about operational and organizational security, the importance of security-related awareness including training, and the role of people in security.

By the end of this chapter, you will be able to

1. Explain the importance of security-related awareness and training.

Security Options

Operations security (OPSEC) means that we are protecting all of the pieces that could be put together to give a clearer vision of the big picture. In the military, OPSEC is the protection of critical information that is mission-essential per military commander.

Operations security also guides the development of the security policies and procedures for an organization. Using encryption software to protect email, being aware of your surroundings, or limiting the amount of information posted on a social media site all contribute to this effort.

© Ahmed F. Sheikh 2020
A. F Sheikh, *CompTIA Security+ Certification Study Guide*, https://doi.org/10.1007/978-1-4842-6234-4_4

Policies guide all of the other components. Upper management is responsible for developing the policies that are used to base all subsequent security measures on. For example, you may purchase a firewall appliance, but how are you going to configure it properly? Policies provide the answer.

For example, an organization establishes a policy that all users must have a unique user ID and password that conforms to the company password standard. Users must not share their password with anyone regardless of title or position. Passwords must not be stored in written or any readable form. If a compromise is suspected, it must be reported immediately to the help desk.

The company standard is that passwords are a minimum of eight upper and lowercase alphanumeric characters including at least one special character. Passwords must be changed every 30 days, and a password history of 12 previous passwords will be maintained to ensure that passwords are not reused for one year.

A guideline is available suggesting that you take a phrase like "I have a dream." Convert this to a strong password such as Ihv@dr3@m. You can then create other passwords from this phrase by changing the number, moving the symbol, or changing the punctuation mark.

The procedure for changing a password is accomplished as follows:

1. Press Ctrl+Alt+Del to bring up the log-in dialog box.

2. Click the "change password" button.

3. Enter your current password in the top box.

4. Enter your new password where indicated.

5. Reenter your new password for verification.

The Operational Process

Once a policy has been developed does not mean that the organization never has to address that need again. The environment may change, and different technologies may emerge, or breaches may occur. An organization must continually look at its security plans, monitor their effectiveness, and evaluate whether changes are necessary (Figure 4-1). Vulnerability assessments or penetration tests are two methods which can be used to ensure that security is adequate.

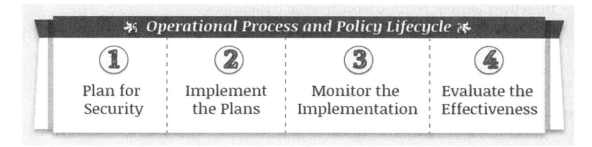

Figure 4-1. *Operational Process and Policy Life Cycle*

1. **Plan for Security**: Develop the policies, procedures, and guidelines that will be implemented, and design the security components that will protect your network.

2. **Implement the Plan**: Deliver instructions on the current plan.

3. **Monitor the Implementation**: Ensure that the hardware and software as well as the policies, procedures, and guidelines are effective in securing your systems.

4. **Evaluate the Effectiveness**: May include vulnerability assessments and penetration tests.

Controls

A security perimeter has several layers of security and creates what is known as defense-in-depth. When you take a look at the various control categories, as mentioned in Figure 4-2, you can see how these controls cover the various layers of security.

❧ Types of Controls ❧				
Directive	Preventative	Detective	Corrective	Recovery

Figure 4-2. *Types of Controls*

Directive Controls: Policies, procedures, and guidelines

Preventive Controls: Passwords, user IDs, and firewalls

Detective Controls: Audit trails, alarms, logs, and surveillance

Corrective Controls: Procedures and manuals

Recovery Controls: Backup, software escrow, insurance, redundancy, equipment, facilities, and contingency plans

Physical Security

Physical security mechanisms are employed to ensure that only authorized users have physical access to computer systems and networks. Physical security should be examined from all six sides—all four walls, the ceiling, and the floor. You can spend a large amount on purchasing and implementing the latest in security technologies, but if you are not diligent about physical proximity to network devices, wiring closets, or server rooms, it will be money spent in futility. Physical security can also be ensured with the help of virtual geo-fencing using RFID tags and anchors. This can help to reduce the deployment cost but cannot be a true replacement of actual physical security.

Physical Barriers

Physical barriers are the first thing that comes to mind when you think of physical security. This is the outermost layer of physical security, and these solutions are the most publicly visible. A prison employs a number of physical barriers listed here. Figure 4-3 includes a list of physical barriers reflective of the principle of layered security: fences, a guard at the gate, open space, walls, signs denoting public and private areas, and/or a man trap.

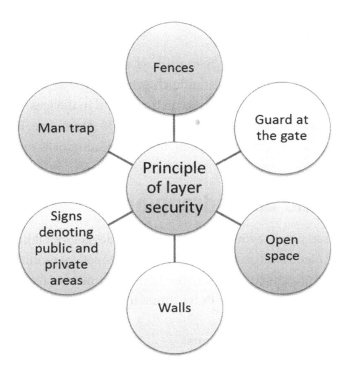

Figure 4-3. *Physical Barriers*

Environmental Issues

Considering various environmental issues may not seem like a security concern, but think what would happen to the servers in the server room should the air conditioning fail. Heating, ventilation, and air conditioning (HVAC) systems for server rooms and equipment closets are important due to the amount of heat generated by the equipment. What would happen to the organization during a power outage? Uninterruptible power supply (UPS) is used for critical systems so that loss of power will not halt processing. It is a fact that electrical power is subject to surges and disruption. Measures must be taken to protect sensitive electronic equipment from fluctuations in voltage.

The frequency of natural disaster is also a contributing factor that needs to be considered when making contingency plans for an organization. Think over the last couple of months. How many natural disasters can you think of?

Fire Suppression

Fire detection and fire suppression devices are ways that can be used to address a fire disaster. For the computer equipment, standard sprinkler-type systems cannot be used since the water will ruin the electrical infrastructure found in devices. Gas-based systems using argon and nitrogen mixing systems are a preferable alternative. Halon was used for many years, but since halon displaces oxygen, the risk to humans is too great.

Electromagnetic Eavesdropping

Electromagnetic eavesdropping sounds very cloak and dagger, but it has been documented that the electromagnetic interference produced by monitors can be picked up and decoded with the right equipment. The US Department of Defense uses the term TEMPEST (**T**ransient **E**lectro**m**agnetic **P**ulse **E**manation **St**andard) to describe electronic emanations from electrical equipment.

Three basic ways to protect emanations

1. Keep equipment at a safe distance.

2. Provide shielding for equipment.

3. Provide shielded enclosure, such as a room.

Distance between the target and the attacker is the simplest way to protect against equipment being monitored. Shielding equipment is also available for purchase, although the cost of shielding is very expensive.

Location

Where you locate equipment can provide an economical solution to any concerns you may have about electronic emanations. Leaving less-sensitive equipment in the areas closest to public areas is one way to accomplish this. Keep the following in mind:

Where equipment is situated can increase or decrease its exposure to risk:

- Where will you place access points?

- How deep in the building can you place sensitive equipment?

- What is the proximity of the building to roads?

- Where are the monitors?

- Where are your printers?

Role of People in Security

There are a number of preventive steps we can take to protect our computers and networks, but humans are the biggest reason why these technologies are not enough. They create security issues through poor practices such as installing unauthorized software, selecting a poor password, and writing down secrets. Most organizations, to prevent any security issues, do not encourage their workers to install any software on their computers.

Social Engineering

Social engineering is a completely nontechnical means for an attacker to get information on his target. We will take a look at the various ways that social engineering can compromise an organization. There are numerous steps that an organization can take to improve security, and one of the ways to accomplish this is to turn the employees into assets rather than liabilities.

Social engineering is using one's "gift of gab" to make another individual let his or her guard down, so to speak, so that he or she divulges information that would not normally be divulged or to take an action that would not normally be taken. It also plays upon the desire of most people to be helpful in the workplace. How many organizations do you know of that emphasize customer service? Information that is gained can sometimes be used directly in an attack, but most times it is used indirectly as part of a more elaborate scheme.

Phishing

Phishing is a type of social engineering that has an attacker masquerading as a trusted entity. See Figure 4-4. For example, you may receive an email from your bank requesting that you verify sensitive information such as your username and password. The bank's logo is part of the email, and the request looks legitimate. When you click on the link provided, though, the web page that opens is not from your bank. The URL may not even be close to that of the bank. It is also important to keep in mind that organizations do not require this type of verification via email.

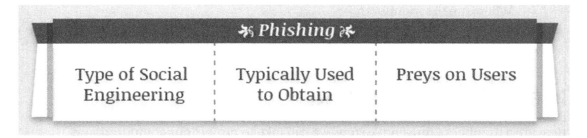

Figure 4-4. *Phishing Purposes*

1. **Type of Social Engineering**: Attacker masquerades as a trusted entity, typically sent to a large group of random users via email or instant messenger

2. **Typically Used to Obtain**: Usernames, passwords, credit card numbers, and details of the user's bank account

3. **Preys on Users**: PayPal, eBay, major banks, and brokerage firms

Spear Phishing and Pharming

Spear phishing targets a group of people with something in common. They may all work for the same company or order merchandise from the same website. The deceptive emails are sent from organizations that the potential victims would normally get email from. Attackers do need some inside information on their targets to convince them that the emails are legitimate.

With pharming, the attacker intends to redirect a website's traffic to another, fake website. To accomplish this, a vulnerability in DNS server software may be exploited, for example. Pharming redirects you automatically to the fake website usually without your knowledge.

Vishing

Vishing is using social engineering over the telephone, and its name comes from the combination of voice plus phishing. Vishing exploits the public's trust in landline telephone service. What most people do not realize is that Voice over IP makes features such as caller ID easy to spoof. Again, the goal here is to gain access to private personal and financial information.

Shoulder Surfing

An attacker can observe, or shoulder surf, to pick up PINSs, access codes, or credit card numbers. An attacker can be in close proximity to his victim, or the attacker can use binoculars or closed-circuit cameras to shoulder surf. You may notice that when you use an ATM, the screen can only be easily read at certain angles. These types of safeguards are put into place to make shoulder surfing much more difficult.

Security Hoaxes

In a lot of instances, a security hoax can cause just as much disruption as a breach would cause. A hoax is designed to elicit a user reaction. There are numerous websites that you can consult to find out if a message is indeed a hoax. Hoax-Slayer1 is one such site. Training and awareness are precautions that can be taken against security hoaxes.

Password Best Practices

Using a password is the most popular way to authenticate. A password is something that you know, and following the best practices guidelines can help you keep your passwords secure. Creating a good password is a balancing act between having a password that cannot easily be cracked with the numerous tools that are available on the Internet vs. a password that is so complex that you have trouble remembering it and are forced to write it down. Review the following recommendations for creating a password:

1.   Use eight or more characters in your password.

2.   Include a combination of upper- and lowercase letters.

3.   Include at least one number and one special character.

4.   Do not use a common word, phrase, or name.

5.   Do not write passwords down.

6.   Think of a phrase, song, poem, or speech that you know by heart.

Piggybacking

If you have someone that you do not know quickly following you into a building because you have a card key, that is piggybacking on your authorized access. Since that individual does not have the proper credentials, you have just given someone unauthorized access to your building.

One of the countermeasures to prevent piggybacking is a man trap. With a man trap, two sets of doors are used. After entering the outer door, that door must be closed before you can enter the inner door.

Dumpster Diving

"One man's trash is another man's treasure." This phrase can be especially true in the world of dumpster diving which is the process of going through a target's trash. Consider securing the trash receptacle. Any sensitive information should be properly disposed of through shredding or the use of burn bags.

Installing Unauthorized Hardware and Software

Many organizations have a policy that restricts users from installing their own software. Consider the following:

- Unauthorized communication software allows users to connect to their machine from their home.

- A wireless access point allows users access to the organization's network from many different areas.

- Installation of games on a company machine can pose security issues.

Installing unauthorized software or hardware can provide a backdoor into the network completely circumventing whatever security measures have been put in place. For example, you may wish to use your wireless tablet device on the company's network, but they do not have a wireless network available. You decide to use a SOHO wireless access point to provide wireless access. You may have unknown vulnerabilities that provide an attacker with the opportunity to breach the organization's network even though the organization has implemented extensive security measures to safeguard its network.

Physical Access by Non-employees

If an organization is lax with its visitor procedures, that can make that organization vulnerable to unauthorized access by a non-employee. Being able to gain physical access is huge for an attacker. Having specific policies that are followed greatly reduces this risk. Keep the following in mind:

- If an attacker can gain physical access, the attacker can penetrate the computer systems and networks.

- Organizations frequently become complacent when faced with a legitimate reason to access the facility.

- Consider personnel who have legitimate access but also have intent to steal intellectual property.

- Physical access provides opportunity for individuals to look for critical information carelessly left out.

- With the proliferation of devices such as cell phones with built-in cameras, an individual could easily photograph information without it being obvious to employees.

Security Awareness

A security awareness program is extremely important for an organization. An employee may not be purposefully malicious but just unaware of what the proper procedures are. A formal training program can be implemented in several different ways from having in-person sessions to offering an online course. Security awareness should also be an ongoing process since new threats and techniques are always on the horizon.

An active security awareness program will vary depending on

- The organization's environment

- The level of threat

A clean desk policy is an example of a safeguard measure that could be implemented. Keeping a workspace clean of information will prevent disclosure to others during casual interactions, and keeping all information secured when not physically present to guard it is a means to prevent compromise in security.

Individual User Responsibilities

It is important to consider that there are several individual user responsibilities that may sound like common sense, but making sure that an individual is aware of these responsibilities helps to promote security awareness in the organization:

1. Lock doors.

2. No sensitive information in your car.

3. Secure storage media containing sensitive information.

4. Shred sensitive documents before discarding.

5. Do not divulge sensitive information to individuals not authorized to know it.

6. Do not discuss sensitive information with family members.

7. Protect laptops that contain the organization's information.

8. Be aware of who is around you when discussing sensitive information.

9. Enforce corporate access control procedures.

10. Report suspected or actual violations of security policies.

11. Follow procedures established to enforce good password security practices.

Roles and Responsibilities

There are some specific terms that are used to illustrate whose responsibility the data of an organization falls under. Data owners, data custodians, and users describe who is responsible for protecting and maintaining data within the organization (Figure 4-5).

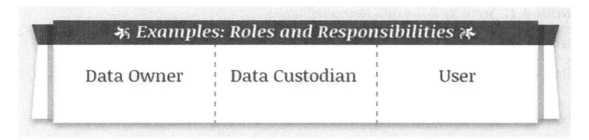

Figure 4-5. *Roles and Responsibilities*

Data Owner: Member of Senior Management responsible for the protection of company assets.

Data Custodian: Responsible for protection and maintenance of data that usually does not belong to them.

User: Any individual who uses company data for their job and who are responsible for the "CIA" Triad.

Security Roles and Responsibilities

Within an organization, there are many different jobs or roles that go into providing a secure work environment for all employees through the establishment of policies, programs, and technologies which safeguard the assets of an organization. In a larger organization, there may actually be an individual that is specifically hired to perform that function. In smaller organizations, though, some of these responsibilities may be assumed by others who wear many hats. To become familiar with the various types of security roles and their responsibilities, review Table 4-1.

Table 4-1. *Security Roles and Responsibilities*

Security role	Responsibility
Chief Technology Officer (CTO)	Identifies and evaluates new technologies and drives new technology development to meet organization objectives
Chief Information Officer (CIO)	Responsible for the information technology and computer systems that support enterprise goals, including successful deployment of new technologies and work processes
Chief Security Officer (CSO)	Develops, implements, and manages the organization's security strategy, programs, and processes associated with all aspects of business operation, including intellectual property
Chief Information Security Officer (CISO)	Responsible for developing and implementing the security policy

Summary

In this chapter you learned about the operational process and policy life cycle, implementing several layers of security and what this entails, and the importance of password protection which included a review of password best practices. Promoting security awareness in the organization is important, and in this lesson, you reviewed individual responsibilities that if implemented could be beneficial. This lesson also provided the opportunity to learn about security roles and responsibilities of individuals within an organization that work to create a secure work environment for all employees by the establishment of policies, programs, and the implementation of technologies used to safeguard assets.

Resources

- **Hoax-Slayer:** www.hoax-slayer.com)/

- **CIA Triad:** www.techrepublic.com/blog/it-security/the-cia-triad/488/

CHAPTER 5

Risk Management

In this chapter you will learn about risk management, vulnerability, and risk assessment. You will gain an understanding of risk-related concepts and risk mitigation strategies.

By the end of this chapter, you will be able to

1. Explain risk related concepts.

2. Apply appropriate risk mitigation strategies.

Risk Management

Risk management is the process of identifying vulnerabilities and threats and their potential impacts. We also need to look at the cost of the countermeasures vs. the cost of the incident itself. A risk assessment can be completed by a qualitative analysis or a quantitative analysis. We will take a look at both. It is important that you have an understanding of the following risk management concepts.

Vulnerabilities

Vulnerability is a weakness that can occur in a number of different ways within an organization. When you think vulnerabilities, having the latest operating system security patches applied or proper software coding may come to mind, but there are a number of areas we can look to for vulnerabilities. Be aware of the following:

- Lack of security understanding

- Misuse of access by authorized users

- Concentration of responsibilities

- Reaction to incidents

- Lack of way to detect fraud

© Ahmed F. Sheikh 2020
A. F Sheikh, *CompTIA Security+ Certification Study Guide*, https://doi.org/10.1007/978-1-4842-6234-4_5

General Risk Management Model

Risk management concepts are fundamentally the same despite their definitions, and they require similar skills, tools, and methodologies. Several models can be used for managing risk through its various phases.

The five steps listed in Figure 5-1 for the general risk management model can be used in virtually any risk management process. Following these steps will lead to an orderly process of analyzing and mitigating risks.

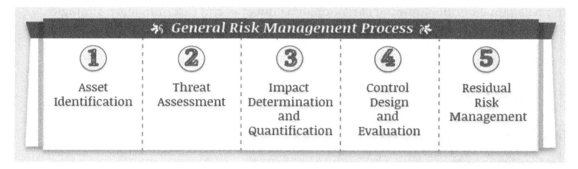

Figure 5-1. *General Risk Management Process*

1. **Asset Identification**: Use a classification that fits the business you are in. Classifying assets will lead to the ability to prioritize assets so that the costs can be properly addressed. The criteria for the classification of assets can be confidentiality, value, time-sensitive, access rights, or destruction to name a few. Asset classification is the key to various security controls that can be implemented for asset protection.

2. **Threat Assessment**: A threat assessment considers a full spectrum of threats including natural, criminal, terrorist, or accidental threats. The assessment should evaluate the likelihood of occurrence for each threat. For natural threats, historical data regarding the frequency of occurrence for each threat can be found.

3. **Impact Determination and Quantification**: When a threat is realized, it turns risk into impact. It is important to determine what the tangible and intangible impacts will be.

Tangible Impact: Results in financial loss

- Direct loss of money

- Loss of business opportunity

- Reduction in operational efficiency or performance

- Interruption of a business activity

Intangible Impact: Hard to quantitatively measure and assigning financial value is difficult

- Breach of legislation or regulatory requirements

- Loss of reputation or goodwill (brand damage)

- Breach of confidence

4. **Control Design and Evaluation**: Countermeasures, or controls, manage risk by reducing vulnerabilities to a level that is considered acceptable. As you can see, a control is considered a preventative control like separation of duties or a detective control such as motion detectors.

   Preventative controls

   - Administrative (policies, separation of duties, security awareness)

   - Physical (swipe cards, locks, alarms)

   - Technical (passwords, encryption, firewalls, antivirus)
     Detective controls

   - Administrative (job rotation, incident response, audits)

   - Technical (IDS, audit logs, forensics)

   - Physical (motion detectors, camera)

5. **Residual Risk Management**: It is important to remember that risk will never completely be eliminated. After you have implemented your controls, you are still left with what is referred to as residual risk. Residual risk is a level of risk that a company can accept to live with. Review Figure 5-2 for a list of potential controls that can be implemented as safeguards.

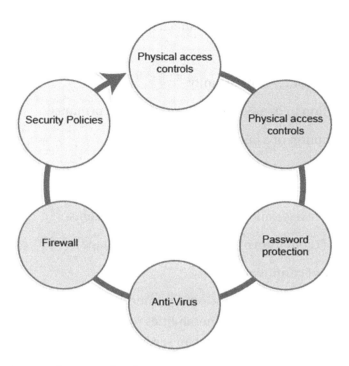

Figure 5-2. *Six Types of Controls That Can Be Implemented As Safeguards*

Qualitatively Assessing Risk

Qualitative risk analysis allows expert judgment and experience to assume a prominent role. To assess risk qualitatively, you compare the impact of the threat with the probability of occurrence and assign an impact level and probability level to the risk. See Table 5-1.

Table 5-1. *Quantitative Risk Assessment*

Impact	Explanation	Weight
Business impact	Would there be a material business impact?	4
Probability of attack	How likely is the attack?	3
Cost to fix	What is the cost and resources required to correct the vulnerability	2
Difficulty to fix	How hard is this to fix from a technical standpoint?	1

For example, if a threat has a high impact and a high probability of occurring, the risk exposure is high and probably requires some action to reduce this threat. Conversely, if the impact is low with a low probability, the risk exposure is low, and no action may be required to reduce this threat.

Note that the matrix shown describes a binary assessment where impact and probability have two possibilities: high or low. In quantitative risk assessments, the goal is to calculate objective numeric values for each component analyzed. The advantage of a quantitative analysis is that there is a dollar figure attached to it which is always an easier sell to upper management.

Annualized Loss Expectancy (ALE)

The annual loss expectancy (ALE) is the total amount of money that an organization will lose in one year if it does nothing to mitigate a risk. To calculate the ALE, determine the single loss expectancy (SLE), and multiply it by the annual rate of occurrence (ARO). The SLE is calculated by multiplying the asset value by the exposure factor. The exposure factor represents a percentage of loss that a threat can have on a particular asset. To estimate the ARO, you can use past experience or the experience of other risk management experts.

The ALE provides a value that an organization can use for budgeting. The ALE helps categorize risks, helps to determine amount to spend on countermeasures, and helps to develop a security budget.

Consider This:

In the example ALE calculation provided here, the resultant ALE provides a dollar amount that can be used to evaluate different countermeasures. If a chosen safeguard costs more than the calculated ALE, you will probably look to alternate solutions.

The first step in calculating ALE is to calculate Single Loss Expectancy (SLE).

- Office building and contents = $2 million
- Exposure factor 50%

SLE = *asset value* * *exposure factor*

SLE = $2 million * 0.5 = $1 million

ALE is then calculated by multiplying SLE by Annualized Rate of Occurrence (ARO).

- ALE = SLE * ARO.

- ARO = 1/20 (1 occurrence every 20 years).

- ALE = $1 million * 1/20 = $50,000.

- The countermeasure to adequately protect this building from complete loss should cost no more than $50,000.

Qualitative vs. Quantitative Risk Assessment

In most cases, risk management will include both qualitative and quantitative elements. Both analysis and judgment or experience will be required. A purely quantitative analysis is virtually impossible as some element of experience will come into play. It is important to consider that it is *impossible* to conduct risk management that is purely quantitative. It is **possible** to accomplish purely qualitative risk management. The decision of whether to use qualitative vs. quantitative risk management depends on the criticality of the project, the resources available, and the management style.

Management's Response

After the team presents the results of the risk assessment to management, management can choose one of four options:

1. **Transfer the Risk**: Third-party involvement.

2. **Reduce the Risk**: Deploy a control.

3. **Accept the Risk**: No further action—informed decision.

4. **Avoid the Risk**: Cease the activity.

If management chooses to accept the risk and do nothing, at least it is an informed decision with backup to support the decision. Many tools, as shown in Figure 5-3, are available to add objectivity and structure throughout the process. Review the various types of available risk management tools.

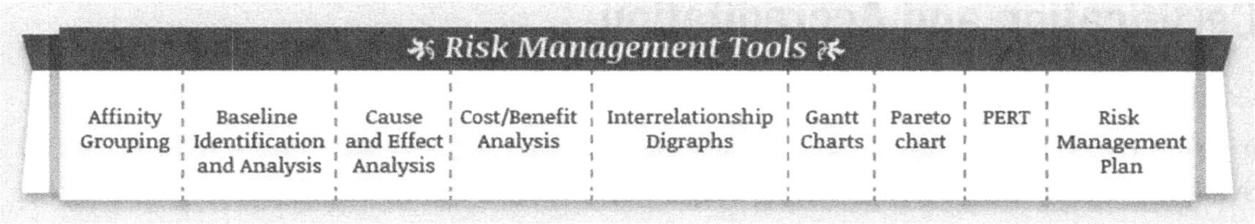

| ⊰ Risk Management Tools ⊱ |
| Affinity Grouping | Baseline Identification and Analysis | Cause and Effect Analysis | Cost/Benefit Analysis | Interrelationship Digraphs | Gantt Charts | Pareto chart | PERT | Risk Management Plan |

Figure 5-3. *Risk Management Tools*

Affinity grouping is a method of identifying items that are related and then identifying the principle that ties them together.

Baseline identification and analysis is the process of establishing a baseline set of risks. It produces a "snapshot" of all the identified risks at a given point in time.

Cause-and-effect analysis is the process of identifying relationships between a risk and the factors that can cause it. This is usually accomplished using fishbone diagrams developed by Dr. Kaoru Ishikawa, former professor of engineering at the Science University of Tokyo.

Cost–benefit analysis is a straightforward method for comparing cost estimates with the benefits of a mitigation strategy.

Interrelationship digraphs are a method for identifying cause-and-effect relationships by clearly defining the problem to be solved, identifying the key elements of the problem, and then describing the relationships between each of the key elements.

Gantt charts are a management tool for diagramming schedules, events, and activity duration.

Pareto chart is a histogram that ranks the categories in a chart from most frequent to least frequent, thus facilitating risk prioritization.

PERT (program evaluation and review technique) charts are diagrams depicting interdependencies between project activities, showing the sequence and duration of each activity. When complete, the chart shows the time necessary to complete the project and the activities that determine that time (the critical path). The earliest and latest start and stop times for each activity and available slack times can also be shown.

Risk management plan is a comprehensive plan documenting how risks will be managed on a given project. It contains processes, activities, milestones, organizations, responsibilities, and details of each major risk management activity and how it is to be accomplished. It is an integral part of the project management plan.

Certification and Accreditation

Certification and Accreditation (C&A) is a process used by the US Federal Government to evaluate, test, and authorize systems before or after the system is in operation. System certifiers and accreditors are responsible for providing certification or assessing management.

Certification: The process of assessing whether all features of an information system (both technical and nontechnical) satisfy minimum security requirements.

- Test the security safeguards.

- Evaluate technical security measures for functionality and assurance.

Accreditation: The official approval to operate an information system for a specific period of time.

- Signifies senior management's approval of the residual risk

Certification and Accreditation Guidelines

The National Institute of Standards and Technology (NIST) Special Publication 800-37, "Guide for Applying the Risk Management Framework to Federal Information Systems," provides a six-step framework for guidance in the Certification and Accreditation (C&A) process:

1. Apply consistent, comparable, and repeatable evaluations of the security controls.

2. Create complete information for authorizing officials.

3. Create a documentation policy of all procedures and controls implemented.

   - System categorization statement document

   - System description document

   - Network diagram and data flows

   - Hardware and software inventory

   - System security plan and risk assessment

   - Contingency plan

Certification and Accreditation Process

The C&A process is outlined in Figure 5-4. The information security plan is now in place, and the C&A process will lead to a security accreditation decision.

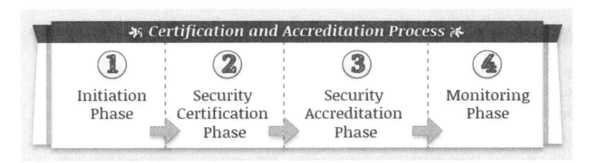

Figure 5-4. *Certification and Accreditation Process*

1. **Initiation Phase**: Security manager is in agreement with the information security plan.

2. **Security Certification Phase**: Security control assessment; security certification documentation.

3. **Security Accreditation Phase**: Security accreditation decision, security accreditation documentation.

4. **Monitoring Phase**: Configuration management and control; security control monitoring; status reporting.

Approval to Operate

An Approval to Operate (ATO) is the formal declaration by a Designated Approving Authority (DAA) that authorizes operation and accepts the residual risks. The ATO is signed after a Certification Agent (CA) certifies that the system meets all requirements.

Official permission is granted by a designated approving authority to operate automated information systems (AISs) or networks in a particular security mode:

- DAA verifies that the residual risk is within acceptable limits.

- DAA ensures that each AIS fulfills the AIS security requirements as reported by the information systems security officer (ISSO).

- Valid for three years.

Interim Approval to Operate

- DAA determines the acceptable level of risk for the system or network to operate at.

- Valid for a maximum of one year.

Approvals

Several agreements are involved in the C&A process and are outlined in Figure 5-5. Since a signed ATO is required prior to full startup, it is the CA's responsibility to start the process early enough to receive the ATO on a timely basis.

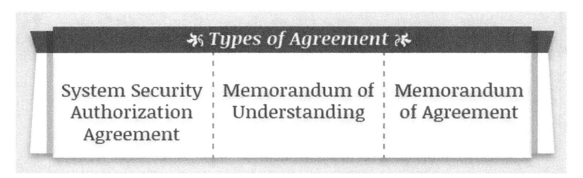

Figure 5-5. *Types of Agreement*

System Security Authorization Agreement: A formal agreement among the DAA, certifier, user representative, and program manager to document decisions, security requirements, certification results, certifier's recommendation, and DAA's approval to operate.

Memorandum of Understanding: A memorandum that describes concepts of mutual understanding, goals, and plans shared by parties.

Memorandum of Agreement: A memorandum that describes the specific responsibilities of and actions to be taken by each party so that their goals can be accomplished.

Summary

In this chapter you learned about risk-related concepts including types of vulnerabilities to be aware of in order to implement appropriate risk mitigation strategies. You also reviewed the general risk management model and the following concepts: how to qualitatively assess risk, the concept of annualized loss expectancy, and the process of completing a qualitative vs. quantitative risk assessment.

CHAPTER 6

Change Management and Disaster Recovery

Change management is a structured approach for performing and recording changes during software development and system operation. In a technology-based environment, change management involves keeping track of the details of the system. Sometimes change management is considered expensive, nonproductive, or unnecessary. In this chapter you will learn about some of the essential elements that make change management an important enterprise management tool.

Additionally, there are many types of disasters that can disrupt an organization's operations. These events can be caused by nature or by people. Although it is more likely that an organization will experience a disruption at some point due to an employee error, a proper disaster plan will prepare the organization for any type of disruption. You will have the opportunity to gain an understanding about recovering from disasters. Backups, alternative site processing, and policies and procedures all play a role.

By the end of this chapter, you will be able to

1. Compare and contrast aspects of business continuity.

2. Execute disaster recovery plans and procedures.

Why Change Management?

Change management is a structured approach for performing and recording changes during software development and system operation. Change management is an essential part of creating a viable governance and control structure and critical compliance with the Sarbanes–Oxley Act.

© Ahmed F. Sheikh 2020
A. F Sheikh, *CompTIA Security+ Certification Study Guide*, https://doi.org/10.1007/978-1-4842-6234-4_6

In a technology-based environment, change management involves keeping track of the details of the system. For example, we would track what operating system release is running on each computer and which fixes have been applied. Sometimes change management is considered expensive, nonproductive, or unnecessary, but we will take a look at some of the essential elements that make change management an important enterprise management tool. Change is considered to be the addition, modification, or removal of anything that could have an effect on information technology services. For example, a module may be modified to a module to implement a new capability.

Here are some of the various types of changes:

Standard change is a preapproved change that is low risk, relatively common, and follows a procedure or work instruction. For example, a small rounding adjustment must be made by finance each month to reconcile the General Ledger to account for foreign currency calculations.

Emergency change is a change that must be introduced as soon as possible such as a fix that resolves a major incident or patches a security concern.

Table 6-1 shows the scenarios and the suggested change management implementations. Each of these scenarios can be controlled, and impacts mitigated, through proper change management procedures.

Table 6-1. *Scenarios and the Suggested Change Management Implementations*

Scenario	Situation	Change management implementation
1	*The developers can't find the latest version of the production source code*	Change management practices support versioning of software changes
2	*A bug corrected a few months ago mysteriously reappears*	*Proper change* management ensures developers always use the most recently changed source code
3	*Fielded software was working fine yesterday but does not work properly today*	*Good change management controls access to previously* modified modules so that previously corrected errors aren't reintroduced into the system
4	*Development team members overwrote each other's changes*	*Today's* change management tools support collaborative development

(continued)

Table 6-1. (*continued*)

Scenario	Situation	Change management implementation
5	*A programmer spent several hours changing the wrong version of the software*	*Change management tools support viable management of* previous software versions
6	*New pricing stored in a table had been overwritten with last year's prices*	*Change control prevents inadvertent overwriting of critical* reference data
7	*A network administrator inadvertently brings down a server as he incorrectly punched down the wrong wires*	Data center connection paths can be version-controlled
8	*A newly installed server is hacked soon after installation because it is improperly configured*	*Network and system administrators use* change management to ensure configurations consistently meet security standards

The Key Concept: Separation of Duties

Separation of duties can be applied in many organizational scenarios because it establishes a basis for accountability and control. Proper separation of duties can safeguard enterprise assets and protect against risks. They should be documented, monitored, and enforced.

A well-understood business example of separation of duties is in the management and payment of vendor invoices. If a person can create a vendor in the finance system, enter invoices for payment, and then authorize a check to be written, it is apparent that fraud could be perpetrated because the person could write a check to himself for services never performed. Separating duties by requiring one person to create the vendors and another person to enter invoices and write checks makes it more difficult for someone to defraud an employer. Information technology (IT) organizations should design, implement, monitor, and enforce appropriate separation of duties for the enterprise's information systems and processes.

Managers at all levels should review existing and planned processes and systems to ensure proper separation of duties. Smaller business entities may not have the resources to implement these practices fully, but other control mechanisms, including hiring qualified personnel, bonding contractors, and using training, monitoring, and evaluation practices, can reduce any organization's exposure to risk.

The establishment of such practices can ensure that enterprise assets are properly safeguarded and can also greatly reduce error and the potential for fraudulent or malicious activities:

- Change management practices implement and enforce separation of duties by adding structure and management oversight to the software development and system operation processes.

- Change management techniques can ensure that only correct and authorized changes, as approved by management or other authorities, are allowed to be made, following a defined process.

Review the steps, shown in Figure 6-1, that can be used to implement separation of duties.

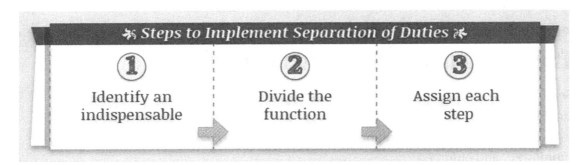

Figure 6-1. *Steps to Implement Separation of Duties*

1. **Identify an indispensable** function that is potentially subject to abuse.

2. **Divide the function** into separate steps, each containing the power that enables the function to be abused.

3. **Assign each step** to a different person or organization.

Elements of Change Management

Change management is the process responsible for controlling the life cycle of all changes. The primary objective of change management is to enable beneficial changes to be made, with minimum disruption to IT services.

Most of today's software and hardware change management practices derive from long-standing system engineering configuration management practices. Computer hardware and software development have also evolved to the point that proper management structure and controls must exist to ensure the products operate as planned.

Change management is commonly referred to as configuration management and includes four general phases: configuration auditing, configuration identification, configuration accounting, and configuration control. See Figure 6-2.

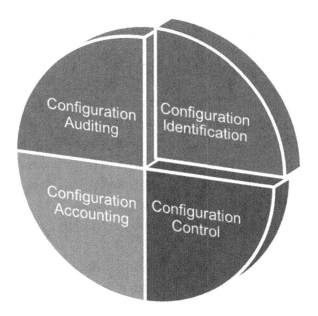

Figure 6-2. Configuration Management Phases

Configuration Identification

Configuration identification is the process of identifying which assets need to be managed and controlled. Configuration identification results in a baseline. This baseline serves as a foundation for comparison or measurement and provides the necessary visibility to control change. For example, a software baseline defines the software system as it is built and running at a point in time.

Configuration Control

Configuration control is an important function of configuration management. Its purpose is to ensure that only approved changes to a baseline are allowed. Configuration identification would include identifying assets such as software modules, test cases, table values, sub-systems, systems, and hardware.

Configuration Status Accounting

For example, it documents what changes have been requested; what changes have been made, when, and for what reason; who authorized the change; who performed the change; and what other configuration items or systems were affected by the change.

Returning to our example of servers being baselined, if the operating system of those servers is found to have a security flaw, then the baseline can be consulted to determine which servers are vulnerable to this particular security flaw.

Those systems with this weakness can be updated (and only those that need to be updated).

Configuration control and configuration status accounting help ensure that systems are more consistently managed and, ultimately in this case, the organization's network security is maintained.

Configuration Auditing

Configuration auditing takes on two forms:

- Functional

- Physical

A functional configuration audit verifies that the configuration item performs as defined by the documentation of the system requirements.

A physical configuration audit confirms that all configuration items to be included in a release, install, change, or upgrade are actually included and that no additional items are included—no more, no less.

Implementing Change Management

Release management is the process responsible for planning, scheduling, and controlling the movement of releases to test live environments. The primary objective of release management is to ensure that the integrity of the live environment is protected and that the correct components are released.

For example, if a threat has a high impact and a high probability of occurring, the risk exposure is high and probably requires some action to reduce this threat (the darkest box). Conversely, if the impact is low with a low probability, the risk exposure is low, and no action may be required to reduce this threat (lighter box).

Note that the matrix shown describes a binary assessment where impact and probability have two possibilities: high or low.

Software Change Control Workflow

This figure shows that developers never have access to the production system or data.

It also demonstrates proper separation of duties between developers, QA and test personnel, and production. It implies that a distinct separation exists between development, testing and QA, and production environments.

This workflow outlined below is for changes that have a major impact on production or the customer's business process.

Change Management Workflow

1. Developer checks source code from the code control tool.

2. Developer modifies the code and conducts unit testing of the changed modules.

3. Developer checks the modified code into the code control tool archive.

4. Developer notifies the buildmaster that changes are ready for a new build and testing/QA.

5. Buildmaster creates a build incorporating the modified code and compiles the code.

6. The buildmaster notifies the system administrator that the executable image is ready for testing/QA.

7. The system administrator moves the executables to the test/QA system.

8. QA tests the new executables. If tests are passed, test/QA notifies the manager. If tests fail, the process starts over.

9. Upon manager approval, the system administrator moves the executable to the production system.

The Purpose of a Change Control Board (CCB)

Figure 6-3 shows the process for implementing and properly controlling hardware or software during changes per the CCB. The CCB convenes on a regular basis, usually weekly or monthly, and can be convened on an emergency or as-needed basis as well.

The CCB's membership should consist of development project managers, network administrators, system administrators, test/QA managers, an information security manager, an operations center manager, and a help desk manager. Others can be added as necessary, depending on the size and complexity of the organization.

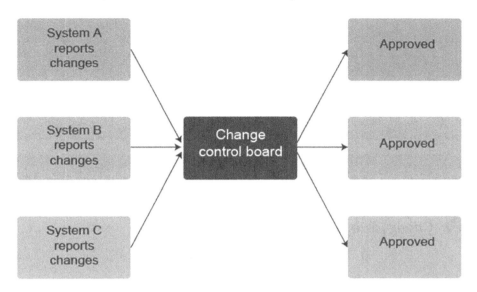

Figure 6-3. *Change Control Board*

The Change Management Process

Figure 6-4 shows the entire change management process and its relationship to incident management and release management. Change management is illustrated in Figure 3 using an example of a Help Desk Ticket:

1. User report to Help Desk, ticket creation.

2. Escalation and assign to team.

3. Assess and quantify.

4. Problem resolution.

5. Close ticket.

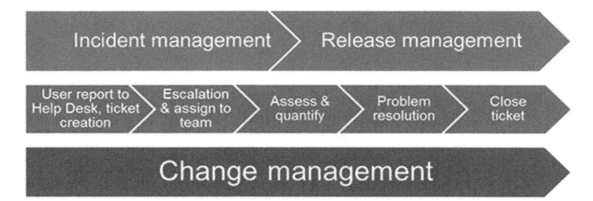

Figure 6-4. *Change Management Process*

Management and Policy Goals

Management's goal is to keep all aspects of its business functioning despite the disruptive events that will inevitably occur. A means to orderly resume operations must be addressed.

Disaster recovery focuses on the technology systems that support those business functions:

- Activities and programs designed to return the entity to an acceptable condition. The ability to respond to an interruption in services by implementing a disaster recovery plan to restore an organization's critical business functions.

Business continuity takes a more long-sighted view of keeping an organization going:

- Deals with longer-term outages

  Focus: Provide methods and procedures.

- Moves critical systems to another environment
  Focus: Sustain an alternate site while the primary site is repaired.

- Conduct business in a different way

  Focus: Get right people to the right place.

- Maintains security

Disaster Recovery Plans (DRP)/Process

To begin creating your DRP, first identify all critical functions and then answer the following questions for each of these critical functions:

- Who is responsible for the operation of this function?

- What do these individuals need to perform the function?

- When should this function be accomplished relative to other functions?

- Where will this function be performed?

- How is the function performed? What is the process?

- Why is this function so important or critical to the organization?

By answering these questions, you can create an initial draft of your organization's DRP. The name often used to describe the document created by addressing these questions is a business impact assessment (BIA). This DRP will need to be approved by management, and it is essential that they buy into the plan—otherwise, your efforts will more than likely fail. A good DRP must include the processes and procedures needed to restore your organization to proper functioning and to ensure continued operation. What specific steps will be required to restore operations? These processes should be documented and, where possible and feasible, reviewed and exercised on a periodic basis. Having a plan with step-by-step procedures that nobody knows how to follow does nothing to ensure the continued operation of the organization. Exercising your disaster recovery plans and processes before a disaster occurs provides you with the opportunity to discover flaws or weaknesses in the plan when there is still time to modify and correct them. It also provides an opportunity for key figures in the plan to practice what they will be expected to accomplish.

DRP Considerations

In developing your BIA and DRP, you may find it useful to categorize the various functions your organization performs, such as shown in Table 6-2. This categorization is based on how critical or important the function is to your business operation and how long your organization can last without the function.

Those functions that are the most critical will be restored first, and your DRP should reflect this. If the function does not fall into any of the first four categories, then it is not really needed, and the organization should seriously consider whether it can be eliminated altogether. See Table 6-2.

Table 6-2. *Categorization of Various Functions*

Category	Level of the function's need	How long can the organization last without the function?
Critical	Absolutely essential for operations. Without the function, the basic mission of the organization cannot occur	The function is needed immediately. The organization cannot function without it
Necessary for normal processing	Required for normal processing, but the organization can live without it for a short period of time	Can live without it for at most 30 days before your organization is severely impacted
Desirable	Not needed for normal processing but enhances the organization's ability to conduct its mission efficiently	Can live without the function for more than 30 days, but it is a function that will eventually need to be accomplished when normal operations are restored
Optional	Nice to have but does not affect the operation of the organization	Not essential, and no subsequent processing will be required to restore this function
Consider eliminating	No discernable purpose for the function	No impact to the organization; the function is not needed for any organizational purpose

Business Continuity Plan (BCP)

Another term that is often used when discussing the issue of continued organizational operations is business continuity plan (BCP). In reality, these two terms are sometimes used synonymously, and for many organizations, there may be no major difference in the two.

The following are key elements of a BCP that are important to recognize:

- Focus on the continued operation of a business in extenuating circumstances.

- Place a strong emphasis on critical systems.

- Describe the functions that are most critical, based on a previously conducted BIA.

- Describe the order in which functions should be returned to operation.

- Describe what is needed for the business to continue to operate.

What Needs to Be Backed Up?

An organized backup plan will not only ensure that your data is safeguarded but that all of the software (like applications, operating systems, and utilities) being used is also accounted for. See Figure 6-5.

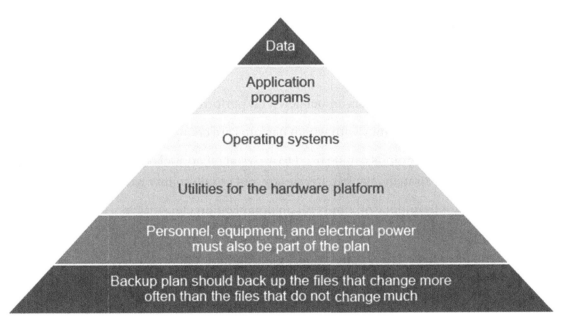

Figure 6-5. *Business Continuity Plan*

Carefully consider the type of backup that you want to conduct. With the size of today's PC hard drives, a complete backup of the entire hard drive can take a considerable amount of time. Implement the type of backup that you need, and check for software tools that can help you in establishing a viable backup schedule.

There are four types of backups. Please review the Table 6-3 for details.

Table 6-3. *Four Types of Backups*

Type	Description	Amount of space	Restoration
Full	All files copied onto the storage media	Large	Simple
Differential	Files that have changed since last full backup	Medium	Simple
Incremental	Files since last full or incremental backup	Medium	Involved
Delta	Portions of files changed since last backup	Small	Complex

Backup strategies are such a critical element of security that you need to make sure you understand the different types of backups and their advantages and disadvantages.

When you are calculating the cost of the backup strategy, consider the following questions:

- What is the cost of the backup media required for a single backup?

- What are the storage costs for the backup media based on the retention policy?

- What are the labor costs associated with performing a single backup?

- What is the frequency with which backups are created?

All of these considerations can be used to arrive at an annual cost for implementing your chosen backup strategy. Backup frequency and retention involve the following:

1. The base frequency on time that an organization can survive without current data

2. The base retention on operational environment and frequency of backups

The following equations can be used to determine costs:

$$(probability\ the\ backup\ is\ needed) \times (cost\ of\ restoring\ with\ no\ backup)$$

$$(probability\ the\ backup\ is\ not\ needed) \times (cost\ of\ the\ backup\ strategy)$$

Alternative Sites

Understanding the differences between hot, warm, and cold sites is fundamental to understanding different business continuity strategies. Make sure that you understand the simple differences between these sites, the primary of which is how soon the alternative site can begin processing your organization's work:

- **Hot Site**: A fully configured environment that can be operational immediately.

- **Warm Site**: A partially configured environment that lacks more expensive computing components.

- **Cold Site**: This site includes basic environmental controls but few computing components.

Utilities

For short-term interruptions, such as what might occur as the result of an electrical storm, uninterruptible power supplies (UPSs) may suffice.

These devices contain a battery that provides steady power for short periods of time—enough to keep a system running should power only be lost for a few minutes or enough to allow administrators to gracefully halt the system or network.

For continued operations that extend beyond a few minutes, another source of power will be required. Generally, this is provided by a backup emergency generator. While backup generators are frequently used to provide power during an emergency, they are not a simple, maintenance-free solution. Generators need to be tested on a regular basis, and they can easily become strained if they are required to power too much equipment.

If your organization is going to rely on an emergency generator for backup power, you must ensure that the system has reserve capacity beyond the anticipated load for the unanticipated loads that will undoubtedly be placed on it.

Secure Recovery

When recovering from an incident, you are going to restore from the least critical to the most critical. This entails

- Providing power, communications, and technical support

- Offering a secure operating environment

- Providing restoration of critical files and data

Cloud Computing

Pushing computing into the cloud may make good business sense from a cost perspective, but doing so does not change the fact that your organization is still responsible for ensuring that all the appropriate security measures are properly in place. Cloud computing allows for the contracting of functions like email and file storage to their parties. Although cloud computing can be more cost-effective, it comes with inherent risks. Asking the following questions is needed to help to consider what safeguard measures must be implemented to pursue cloud computing:

- How are backups being performed?

- What plan is in place for disaster recovery?

- How frequently are systems patched? What is the service-level agreement (SLA) associated with the systems?

High Availability and Fault Tolerance

It is important to understand the various ways that a single point of failure can be addressed. These include various types of redundancy as well as high availability clusters.

High availability refers to the ability to maintain availability of data and operational processing despite a disrupting event. Generally, this requires redundant systems, in terms of both power and processing so that should one system fail, the other can take over operations without any break in service. High availability is more than data redundancy; it requires that both data and services be available

Fault tolerance basically has the same goal as high availability—the uninterrupted access to data and services—and is accomplished by the mirroring of data and systems. Should a "fault" occur, causing disruption in a device such as a disk controller, the mirrored system provides the requested data with no apparent interruption in service to the user. High availability clustering is another method used to provide redundancy in critical situations. These clusters consist of additional computers upon which a critical process can be started if the cluster detects that there has been a hardware or software problem on the main system.

A single point of failure is a critical operation in the organization upon which many other operations rely and which itself relies on a single item that, if lost, would halt this critical operation. A single point of failure can be a special piece of hardware, a process, a specific piece of data, or even an essential utility. Single points of failure need to be identified if high availability is required because they are potentially the "weak links" in the chain that can cause disruption of the organization's operations. Generally, the solution to a single point of failure is to modify the critical operation so that it does not need to rely on this single element or need to build redundant components into the critical operation to take over the process should one of these points fail. See Figure 6-6.

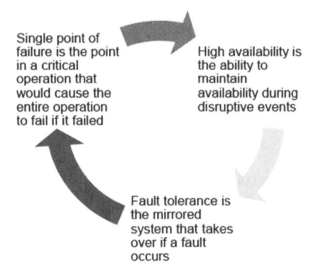

Single point of failure is the point in a critical operation that would cause the entire operation to fail if it failed

High availability is the ability to maintain availability during disruptive events

Fault tolerance is the mirrored system that takes over if a fault occurs

Figure 6-6. *High Availability and Fault Tolerance*

Increasing Reliability

A relatively new approach to increasing reliability in disk storage is the Redundant Array of Inexpensive Disks, now known as Redundant Array of Independent Disks (RAID).

- RAID takes data that is normally stored on a single disk and spreads it out among several others. If any single disk is lost, the data can be recovered from the other disks where the data also resides. With the price of disk storage decreasing, this approach has become increasingly popular to the point that many individual users even have RAID arrays for their home systems.

- RAID can also increase the speed of data recovery as multiple drives can be busy retrieving requested data at the same time instead of relying on just one disk to do the work.

See Figure 6-7 for an example of Raid 1.

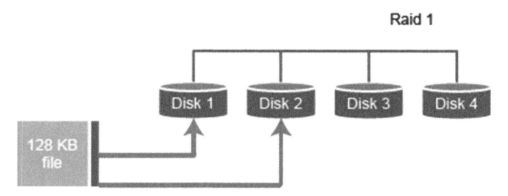

Figure 6-7. *Graphic Represents an Example of Raid 1 to Show Data Being Stored on Multiple Disks*

There are several varieties of RAID from RAID 0 to RAID 6. The following information will provide you with some basic knowledge about RAID 0, RAID 1, and RAID 5.

RAID 0: No Redundancy/Improved Performance

Spreading data out to speed access but with no redundancy to improve reliability and RAID 1 implementing exact copies of disks so that all data is mirrored on another drive providing complete redundancy.

RAID 1: Mirrored Drives/Expensive

Since RAID 1 is extremely expensive (doubling all hardware requirements), other variations of RAID have been developed to provide both reliability and increased speed.

RAID 5: Spread Across Disks with Parity/Inexpensive Redundancy

RAID 5, for example, spreads data across disks and adds parity in a manner such that the loss of any single disk in the array will not result in the loss of any data. These several varieties of RAID can be used together in different combinations to create RAID 10, RAID 01, RAID 03, and RAID 50.

Please see Figure 6-8 for common applications of redundancy.

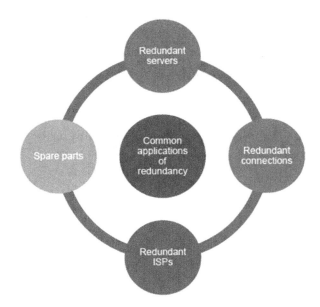

Figure 6-8. *Common Applications of Redundancy*

Computer Incident Response Team (CIRT)

The Computer Incident Response Team, or CIRT, should consist of not only permanent but also ad hoc members who may be called upon to address special needs depending on the nature of the incident. In addition to individuals with a technical background, the CIRT should include nontechnical personnel to provide guidance on ways to handle media attention, legal issues that may arise, and management issues regarding the continued operation of the organization. The CIRT should be created and team members notified before an incident occurs. Policies and procedures for conducting an investigation should also be worked out in advance of an incident occurring. It is also advisable to have the team periodically meet to review these procedures.

Test, Exercise, and Rehearse

Exercises are an often-overlooked aspect of security. The simplest is a tabletop exercise in which participants sit around a table with a facilitator who supplies information related to the "incident" and processes that are being examined. No actual processes or procedures are invoked; they are just discussed. This may result in the realization that a certain type of incident is not currently covered in existing plans.

Another type of exercise is a functional test in which certain aspects of a plan are tested to see how well they work (and how well-prepared personnel are). At the most extreme are full operational exercises designed to actually interrupt services in order to verify that all aspects of a plan are in place and sufficient to respond to the type of incident that is being simulated.

Disaster recovery plans should be practiced periodically as they reveal potential flaws in the plan. See Figure 6-9.

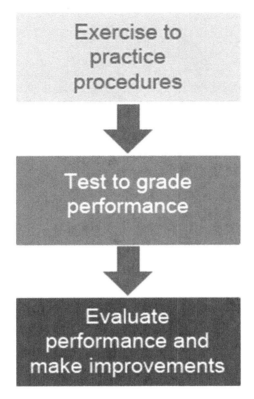

Figure 6-9. *Disaster Recovery Process*

Service-Level Agreement

A service-level agreement (SLA) is a contractual agreement between entities describing specified levels of service that the servicing entity agrees to guarantee for the customer. These agreements not only clearly lay out expectations in terms of the service provided and support expected but also generally include penalties should the described level of service or support not be provided.

   An organization contracting with a service provider should include in the agreement a section describing the service provider's responsibility in terms of business continuity and disaster recovery. The provider's backup plans and processes for restoring lost data should also be clearly described. See Figure 6-10 for an illustration outlining the process of a service-level agreement.

Figure 6-10. *Service-Level Agreement Steps*

Just as with many other disciplines, there is a code of ethics for information technology personnel to keep in mind: principles, employee conduct, values, and integrity.

Incident Response Policies and Procedures

Incident response procedures should also clearly delineate steps in these phases, as the time to decipher and interpret management intentions needs to be during policy and procedure development, not during execution. Most incident response events are time-sensitive, and the procedures should be clear and easy to follow to ensure that all steps are properly taken. See Figure 6-11.

❧ Policies and Procedures ❧				
Preparation	Detection	Containment and Eradication	Recovery	Follow-up Actions

Figure 6-11. *Policies and Procedures*

1. **Preparation**

   - Determine points of contact.

   - Train employees for understanding.

   - Establish the incident response team.

   - Acquire needed equipment.

   - Complete and specialized training needed.

2. **Detection**

   - Determine if an incident has occurred.

   - Work with network and system administrators.

3. **Containment and Eradication**

   - Contain the intruder; decide about prosecution.

   - Restore operations without destroying evidence.

   - Take steps to prevent future incidents (patching, etc.).

4. **Recovery**

   - Assess the situation.

   - Begin recovery based on assessment.

   - Return business back to normal operation.

5. **Follow-Up Actions**

   - Report incident to senior management including what and how
     the incident occurred.

   - Give recommendation to prevent future incidents.

Summary

In this chapter you learned about the change management model. You had the opportunity to review scenarios and the associated change management implementations to help you gain a better application of the change management model concepts. You had the opportunity to learn about the importance of separating duties in order to establish a basis for accountability and control. Additionally, you reviewed the elements of change management, disaster recovery plans including considerations involved in implementing such a plan, and incident response policies and procedures.

Resources

- **Sarbanes-Oxley Act**: `http://searchcio.techtarget.com/definition/Sarbanes-Oxley-Act`

- **Separating duties**: `www.csoonline.com/article/2123120/separation-of-duties-and-it-security.html`

CHAPTER 7

Physical Security

Every day you lock the door to your house as you head out or you lock your car door after you have parked. You may also have an alarm system. You may take these precautions because you are taking steps to protect your possessions and your family. Locks are the most common means of achieving physical security. Physical security is also an important consideration for a business. In this chapter you will learn about many assets that a business may need to secure.

By the end of this chapter, you will be able to

1. Explain the impact of physical security on computer and network security.

2. Explain the impact and proper use of environmental controls.

The Security Problem

If an organization does not take the necessary steps to protect the perimeter, all of the other technology that it deploys will not matter. Physical access negates all other security measures. With the popularity of a universal serial bus (USB) or flash drives, it would not be much of a logistical problem for an attacker to install malware on a system that he has physical access to. See Figure 7-1.

© Ahmed F. Sheikh 2020

A. F Sheikh, *CompTIA Security+ Certification Study Guide*, https://doi.org/10.1007/978-1-4842-6234-4_7

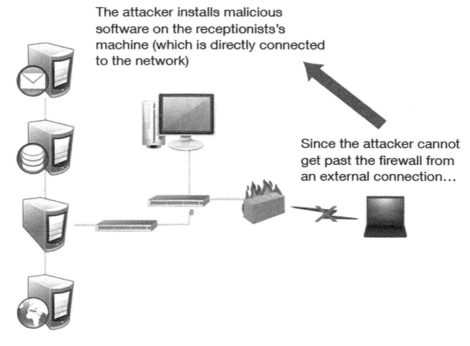

The attacker installs malicious
software on the receptionists's
machine (which is directly connected
to the network)

Since the attacker cannot
get past the firewall from
an external connection...

Figure 7-1. *Physical Security Example*

Bootdisks

A bootdisk is any media (Figure 7-2) used to boot a computer into an operating system
(OS) that is not the native OS on its hard drive.

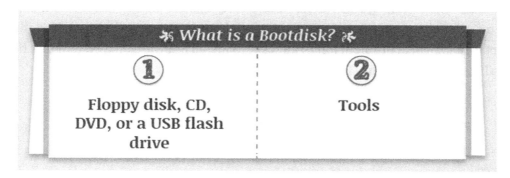

Figure 7-2. *What Is a Bootdisk?*

1. **Floppy Disk, CD, DVD, or a USB Flash Drive**: A bootdisk can be a floppy disk, CD, DVD, or a USB flash drive. Once an attacker is able to read a hard drive, the password file can be copied off the machine for offline password-cracking attacks. If write access to the drive is obtained, the attacker could alter the password file or place a remote control program to be executed automatically upon the next boot, guaranteeing continued access to the machine.

   Most new machines do not include floppy drives, so this attack is rapidly being replaced by the same concept with a CD or DVD. USB devices offer a wide range of size and form factors and are commonly used. Leaving a USB stick out in the open for a passerby to pick up and use is a "road apple" attack. USB drives are portable and easy to conceal.

2. **Tools**: Tools such as scanners, sniffers, drive imagers, and password crackers are just a few examples of programs that can be contained on a USB drive. If an organization lacks physical security solutions to prevent physical access to computers, servers, and other network resources, all the other measures implemented will not be effective.

Once an attacker is able to read a hard drive, the password file can be copied off the machine for offline password-cracking attacks. If write access to the drive is obtained, the attacker could alter the password file or place a remote control program to be executed automatically upon the next boot, guaranteeing continued access to the machine.

Drive Imaging

Physical access is the most common way of imaging a drive, and the biggest benefit for the attacker is that drive imaging leaves absolutely no trace of the crime. Besides physically securing access to your computers, you can do very little to prevent drive imaging. But you can minimize its impact. The use of encryption even if it is only for a few important files provides protection. Full encryption of the drive protects all files stored on it. Alternatively, placing files on a centralized file server keeps them from being imaged from an individual machine. But if an attacker is able to image the file server, the data will be copied.

Many of the methods mentioned so far can be used to perform a denial-of-service (DoS) attack. Physical access to the computers can be much more effective than a network-based DoS attack. Stealing a computer, using a bootdisk to erase all data on the drives, or simply unplugging computers are all effective DoS attacks. Depending on the company's quality and frequency of backing up critical systems, a DoS attack can have a devastating effect. Physical access can negate almost all the security that the network attempts to provide.

Review the following key terms associated with the process of imaging a drive:

- **Use**: Drive imaging is used to perform forensic investigations of computers.

- **Data**: Imaging a drive includes every bit of data that is on the computer including any locally stored documents and emails.

- **Encryption**: Full encryption of the drive protects all files stored on it.

Physical Security Measures

Walls provide barriers to physical access to company assets. Less obvious entry points should also be considered: Is a drop ceiling used in the server room? Do the interior walls extend to the actual roof, raised floors, or crawl spaces? Access to the server room should be limited to the people who need access, not to all employees of the organization. See Figure 7-3. If you are going to use a wall to protect an asset, make sure no obvious holes appear in that wall.

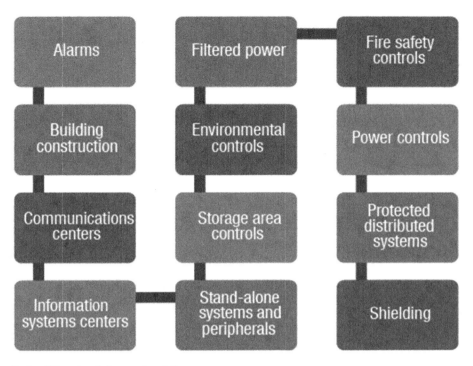

Figure 7-3. *Physical Security Measures*

Computer Policies

To mitigate the risk to computers, physical security needs to be extended to the computers themselves. To combat the threat of bootdisks, begin by removing or disabling the floppy drive from any desktop system that has but does not require it. A DVD not only can be used as a boot device but also can be exploited via the autorun feature that some operating systems support. Some users will undoubtedly insist on having DVD drives in their machines, but, if possible, the drives should be removed from every machine.

Users are often mentioned as the weakest link in the security chain, and that can also apply to physical security. Fortunately, in physical security, users are often one of the primary beneficiaries of the security itself. A security program protects a company's information assets, but it also protects the people of the organization. A good security program will provide tangible benefits to employees, helping them to support and reinforce the security program.

Users need to be aware of security issues, and they need to be involved in security enforcement. Review the steps provided which include computer policies that can be implemented as safeguard measures.

Step 1: Remove or disable the floppy disk system.

Step 2: Remove or disable the optical drive system. If that is not possible, remove the device from the boot menu, and set a BIOS password.

Step 3: Disallow USB drive keys which can be done through active directory or registry settings or by implementing aggressive anti-malware scanning.

Step 4: Lock up equipment that contains sensitive data.

Step 5: Train all employees to lock workstations before leaving them, to challenge strangers, and to follow procedures.

Physical Security Safeguards: Access Controls and Monitoring

Controlling all of the entry points means using access control, screening, and monitoring system to secure a building and its surroundings. Access control systems limit those who can enter, screening systems limit where they can enter, and monitoring systems observe. Access controls include locks, layered access systems, electronic door control systems, and close-circuit television (CCTV). See Figure 7-4.

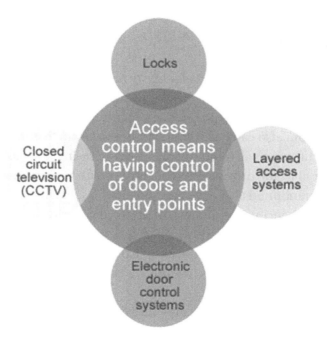

Figure 7-4. *Access Controls*

Layered Access

Servers should be placed in a separate secure area, ideally with a separate authentication mechanism. For example, if an organization has an electronic door control system using contactless access cards as well as a keypad, a combination of the card and a separate PIN code would be required to open the door to the server room.

Many organizations use electronic access control systems to control the opening of doors. Doorways are electronically controlled via electronic door strikes and magnetic locks. These devices rely on an electronic signal from the control panel to release the mechanism that keeps the door closed. These devices are integrated into an access control system that controls and logs entry into all the doors connected to it, typically through the use of access tokens.

Security is improved by having a centralized system that can instantly grant or refuse access based upon a token that is given to the user. This kind of system also logs user access, providing nonrepudiation of a specific user's presence in a controlled environment. The system will allow logging of personnel entry, auditing of personnel movements, and real-time monitoring of the access controls. Keep in mind the following key factors relating to layered access:

- Access to the server room should be limited to staff with a legitimate need to work on the servers.

- Area surrounding the server room should also be limited to people who need to work in that area.

Laptops and Mobile Devices

Laptops and mobile devices require special consideration due to the portable nature of the device. How will you protect a laptop from being lost or stolen? Security cables provide a cost-effective solution. Keep a laptop locked up and out of sight, especially when leaving the office for the evening. Also, make sure that users know what their responsibilities for the laptop are by having a policy in place that all employees are made aware of.

Closed-Circuit Television (CCTV)

Traditional cameras are analog-based and require a video multiplexer to combine all the signals and make multiple views appear on a monitor.

IP-based cameras are stand-alone units viewable through a web browser. These IP-based systems add useful functionality, such as the ability to check on the building from the Internet. This network functionality, however, makes the cameras subject to normal IP-based network attacks.

A DoS attack launched at the CCTV system just as a break-in is occurring is the last thing that anyone would want. For this reason, IP-based CCTV cameras should be placed on their own physically separate network that can be accessed only by security personnel.

The same physical separation applies to any IP-based camera infrastructure. IP-based cameras are not as secure as CCTV and are vulnerable to DoS attacks. They can also be used to launch DDoS attacks on other systems.

Environmental Controls

Maintaining a data center means addressing the airflow and temperature. Overheating of the equipment can result in reduced performance or equipment damage. Temperatures of 70–74° with a humidity range of 40–55% and a minimal dew point of 15° are optimal. Accurate and comprehensive monitoring of environmental support equipment and in-room conditions is extremely important in a sensitive data center environment.

Heating, Ventilating, and Air Conditioning (HVAC) Systems Are Critical for Keeping Data Centers Cool

- Typical servers put out between 1000 and 2000 BTUs of heat.

- The failure of HVAC systems for any reason is cause for concern.

- Properly securing these systems is important in helping prevent an attacker from performing a physical DoS attack on your servers.

Fire Suppression Systems

Since computer rooms or wiring closets are filled with electrical components, a water-based sprinkler system is not going to be the optimum solution. Halon-based fire suppression systems were commonly used, but halon is dangerous for humans. An alternative gas-based system using $CO2$ or some other environmentally friendly clean agent works by absorbing heat, not oxygen. A lot of times, local fire code requires that a water sprinkler system provide backup.

Handheld Fire Extinguishers

Each type of fire has its own fuel source and method for extinguishing it. Class A systems are designed to extinguish fires with normal combustible material as the fire's source. Water can be used in an extinguisher of this sort, since it is effective against fires of this type. Using a Class A extinguisher against an electrical fire will not only be ineffective but can result in additional damage.

Some extinguishers are designed to be effective against more than one type of fire, such as the common ABC fire extinguishers. This is probably the best type of system to have in a data processing facility. All fire extinguishers should be easily accessible and should be clearly marked.

Before anybody uses an extinguisher, they should know what type of extinguisher it is and what the source of the fire is. When in doubt, evacuate and let the fire department handle the situation. Please see Table 7-1 which provides details for each class of extinguisher.

Table 7-1. *Types of Fires and Suppression Methods*

Class	Type of fire	Example of materials	Suppression method
A	Common combustion	Wood, paper, cloth, plastics	Water or dry chemical
B	Combustible liquids	Petroleum products, organic solvents	CO2 or dry chemical
C	Electrical	Electrical wiring and equipment, power tools	CO2 or dry chemical
D	Flammable metals	Magnesium, titanium	Copper metal or sodium chloride

Fire Detection Devices

Although individuals are often familiar with smoke-activated detectors traditionally found in homes, it is important to be aware of the different types of fire detectors that are also available. There are three types of fire detectors. The first relies on temperature change and is heat activated, and the others rely on the flames from a fire.

Review each type of fire detector for specific details.

Smoke-Activated

- Ionization detects ionized particles caused by fire.

- Photoelectric detects degradation of light from smoke.

Heat-Activated

- Fixed temperature alerts if temperature exceeds a predefined level.

- Rate-of-rise temperature detects sudden increases in temperature.

Flame-Activated

- Relies on the flames from the fire to provide a change in the infrared energy that can be detected.

Authentication

Electronic access control systems arose from the need to have more logging and control. Most electronic systems currently use a token-based card that if passed near a reader, and if you have permission from the system, will unlock the door and let you pass into the area. Newer technology attempts to make the authentication process easier and more secure.

Authentication can traditionally be separated into four broad categories: something you have, something you are, something you know, and, less utilized, somewhere you are. Tokens are examples of something you have, biometrics measure something you are, and password-style systems demonstrate something you know. The somewhere you are is more complicated; at a basic level, it prohibits two logins from different areas or the login from a country or location you could not possibly be in. The combination of two or more of these systems is known as multiple-factor authentication. See Figure 7-5.

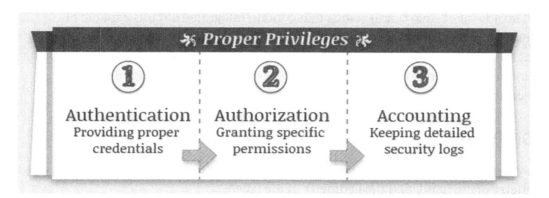

Figure 7-5. *Proper Privileges*

1. **Authentication**: You must provide the proper credentials (like a username and a password) to be authenticated.

2. **Authorization**: You must have authorization. The username you use has specific permissions granted to it.

3. **Accounting**: A log can be used to keep track of what that user account is doing on the network.

Access Tokens

Although keys have been used to unlock devices for centuries, they do have several limitations. Keys are paired exclusively with a lock or a set of locks, and they are not easily changed. It is easy to add an authorized user by giving the user a copy of the key, but it is far more difficult to give that user selective access unless that specified area is already set up as a separate key. It is also difficult to take access away from a single key or key holder, which usually requires a rekey of the whole system.

In many businesses, physical access authentication has moved to contactless radio frequency cards and readers. When passed near a card reader, the card sends out a code using radio waves. The reader picks up this code and transmits it to the control panel. The control panel checks the code against the reader from which it is being read and the type of access the card has in its database.

One of the advantages of this kind of token-based system is that any card can be deleted from the system without affecting any other card or the rest of the system. The tokens themselves can also be grouped in multiple ways to provide different access levels to different groups of people.

The advent of smart cards (cards that contain integrated circuits capable of generating and storing cryptographic keys) has enabled cryptographic types of authentication. The risk of theft of the token can be offset by the use of multiple-factor authentication. One of the ways that people have tried to achieve multiple-factor authentication is to add a biometric factor to the system.

Biometrics

Many biological factors can be used in biometrics, such as the retina or iris of the eye, the geometry of the hand, and the geometry of the face:

- When biometrics is used for authentication, there is a two-part process: enrollment and then authentication. During enrollment, a computer takes the image of the biological factor and reduces it to a numeric value.

- When the user attempts to authenticate, their feature is scanned by the reader, and the computer compares the numeric value being read to the one stored in the database.

- If they match, access is allowed. Since these physical factors are unique, theoretically only the actual authorized person would be allowed access.

There are a few anomalies associated with biometric authentication. The charts, Figures 7-6 and 7-7, illustrate a false-positive and a false-negative condition. How should an organization handle such situations? This is just another example of the procedures that need to be thought out. It is important to consider issues such as a uniqueness factor can be stolen and parts of the human body can change.

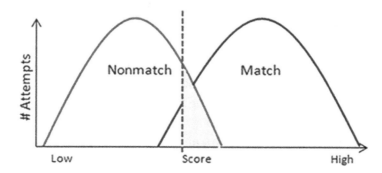

Figure 7-6. *False-Positive: A Biometric Is Scanned and Allows Access to Someone Who Is Not Authorized*

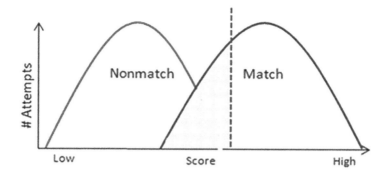

Figure 7-7. *False-Negative: The System Denies Access to Someone Who Is Actually Authorized*

Multiple-Factor Authentication

Multiple-factor authentication combines two or more types of authentication.

Types of authentication include

- **Biometrics**

- **Tokens**

- **Passwords**

For example, you may have an ATM card which you use to take money out of your bank account. This transaction uses multiple-factor authentication. First, you need to insert your ATM card (token) and then you need to enter the PIN (a password). An example of biometrics would be gaining access by using your fingerprint.

Summary

In this chapter you learned about multiple response procedures and methods for how to deal with physical security. You reviewed concepts relating to computer forensics, the incident response model, and the basics of how to procure evidence. In this chapter you also had the opportunity to learn about various types of malware and physical security safeguards including access controls and monitoring.

CHAPTER 8

Forensics, Legal Issues, and Privacy

In this chapter you will learn about various response procedures and methods for appropriately dealing with incidents. You will gain an understanding of computer forensics, the incident response model, along with how to procure evidence. This chapter will also provide you with the opportunity to learn about specific laws which guide the policies and procedures to ensure compliance.

By the end of this chapter, you will be able to

1. Apply appropriate incident response procedures.

2. Identify the various laws that affect cybersecurity.

Computer Forensics

Computer forensics deals with legal evidence found on computers and storage media. The goal is to examine the digital media to identify, preserve, recover, analyze, and present facts about the information. The evidence found by using forensics technologies must follow the rules of evidence that are used for any criminal investigation to create a legal audit trail.

Computer forensics is usually associated with the investigation of computer crimes. This discipline is also used in civil proceedings as well as data recovery.

Computer forensics is used in three situations to

- Investigate a computer system related to a violation of the law.

- Investigate a computer system for compliance with policies.

- Investigate a computer system that has been remotely attacked.

© Ahmed F. Sheikh 2020
A. F Sheikh, *CompTIA Security+ Certification Study Guide*, https://doi.org/10.1007/978-1-4842-6234-4_8

Incident Response Cycle

Since computer forensics investigations can sometimes lead to a court proceeding, use the incident response cycle as a guide to remembering the key steps in computer forensics. An incident is an event outside of the norm and can usually be attributed to a human root cause.

Many organizations have an incident response team made up of individuals from various areas within the organization that can assess the incident and make decisions as to the proper course of action. See Figure 8-1.

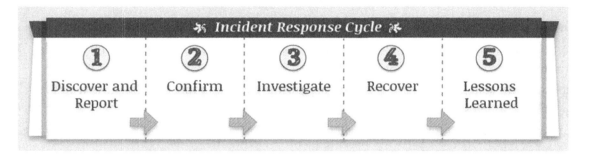

Figure 8-1. *Incident Response Cycle Steps*

1. **Discover and Report**: Administer an incident response reporting process.

2. **Confirm**: Specialists review incident report and confirm occurrence.

3. **Investigate**: Response team investigates incident in detail.

4. **Recover**: Systems and applications returned to operational status.

5. **Lessons Learned**: Action items to correct weaknesses and make improvements.

Evidence

Evidence includes the documents, testimony, and exhibits that are admissible in a court of law. Computer evidence is a challenge due to the fact that data is just a series of bits on a storage media. Evidence must be convincing, it must be legally qualified, and it must be material to the case. As evidence is collected, it is important to note who collected the evidence, how the evidence was collected and from where, and who had possession of the evidence. See Table 8-1 for details regarding standards of evidence.

Table 8-1. *Standards of Evidence and Their Description*

Standards of evidence	Description
Sufficient evidence	Must be convincing or measure up without question
Competent evidence	Must be legally qualified and reliable
Relevant evidence	Must be material to the case or have bearing on the matter at hand

There are several types of evidence as noted. Some types of evidence are stronger than others:

1.   **Direct evidence** is knowledge gained through direct observation.

2.   **Real evidence** is tangible objects that prove or disprove a fact.

3.   **Documentary evidence** consists of business records, printouts, manuals, etc.

4.   **Demonstrative evidence** includes models, charts, and experiments used to aid a jury.

When a judge admits an item in a case, it becomes evidence. There are several US laws that have to do with the gathering of evidence. Computer-generated evidence usually falls into the hearsay rule category. See the following items for details on rules pertaining to evidence:

Best Evidence Rule: Original evidence preferred over duplicates.

Exclusionary Rule: Must have been gained in accordance with all laws.

Hearsay Rule: Secondhand evidence may not be allowed; important as most computer-generated evidence is classified as secondhand.

Now that you have learned about the different types of evidence, it is important to be aware of basic guidelines for procuring evidence. Evidence must be properly acquired, identified, protected, transported, and stored to ensure credibility. Acquiring evidence will require that data be gathered as quickly as possible as the attacker may attempt to cover his or her tracks and/or data may be tampered with or destroyed.

Volatility of Data

Data can be available at a number of stages. Data that is being processed via the CPU is the most volatile and therefore the hardest to capture. You should always use tools and utilities that are not provided as part of the system that you are working on. A forensic workstation is the best solution here.

Data ranging from most volatile to most persistent: CPU storage (registers/cache, system storage (RAM), kernel tables, fixed media, removable media, and output/hardcopy. See Figure 8-2.

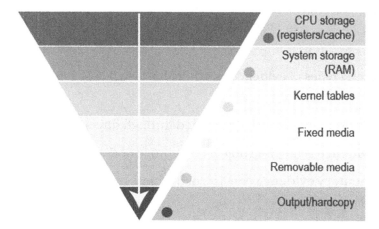

Figure 8-2. *Volatility of Data*

Identifying Evidence

Do not open any files or start any applications. Try to document the current memory and swap files, running processes, and open files. Disconnect the system from the network. Capture any email, Domain Name Service, or any other network service logs on servers. See Table 8-2.

Table 8-2. *Identifying Evidence Methodology*

Tips	Action
Marking evidence	Be methodical
	Work in teams rather than individually
	Keep thorough logs during seizure and analysis
Record-keeping	Identifies the who, what, when, where, and why related to the collected evidence

Safeguarding Evidence

Safeguarding evidence including protecting evidence and ensuring proper transportation of evidence are important considerations. Protect evidence from any temperature extremes, and keep in mind other factors such as humidity, magnetic fields, and vibration. When transporting evidence, remember that a chain of custody must be maintained. There should be no questions as to who handled the evidence or where it was. It is imperative that evidence is properly logged in and out of a controlled storage area and that evidence is properly packaged.

How you store digital evidence can play a big factor in its validity. Digital evidence is often questioned as to its authenticity since it can be easily modified. Plastic materials should not be used to store evidence because plastic can produce or convey static electricity. Consider storing evidence in static-free bags, foam packing material, or cardboard boxes. Leave all mobile devices or smart phones in the power state in which they were found. For those devices that are on, you will need packaging that properly blocks the signal and shields the device from being altered. An evidence room should have restricted access, entry-logging capability, and camera monitoring.

Conducting the Investigation

When conducting an investigation, it is important to consider the following: never analyze the seized system directly, keep thorough and precise notes of all action, and control the environment of the investigation. Analysts use several different tools during their investigation. Forensic workstations are specialized workstations that contain the hardware, software, and components to successfully perform computer forensic investigations. Forensic programs that analyze disk space, file content, and system configuration are part of the forensic workstation. Other tools of the trade include disk wipe utilities, file viewers, hard drive tools, and tools used to recover deleted files.

Steps in Chain of Custody

The chain of custody shows who obtained the evidence, where the evidence was obtained, the time the evidence was obtained, where it was stored, and who had control of the evidence since the time it was obtained. The steps in the chain of custody must be carefully followed to avoid allegations of tampering.

Step 1: Record each item collected as evidence.

Step 2: Write a description of it in the documentation.

Step 3: Store evidence in labeled containers.

Step 4: Record all hash values in the documentation.

Step 5: Securely transport evidence to the storage facility.

Step 6: Obtain signature of the person who accepts it.

Step 7: Provide controls to prevent access to it.

Step 8: Securely transport evidence to court.

Understanding Drive Space Allocation

Stored digital evidence provides some unique opportunities. It is important to understand both free space and slack space regarding drive space allocation. Please see Table 8-3.

When you delete a file, the pointer in the file allocation table used by the operating system is removed. The actual file contents still remain on the storage media. The operating system can reuse the clusters taken up by the deleted file, if needed. There are a number of tools which can be used to look at those clusters.

Slack space occurs when a file is saved to storage media; the operating system allocates that space in blocks that are a predefined size (clusters). For very small files, the operating system will allocate one cluster for storage. The leftover space in the cluster is referred to as slack space.

Table 8-3. *Drive Space Allocation*

Drive Space	Description
Free	Memory cluster marked as usable by the OS
	May contain fragment of previously deleted file
	Is allocated when OS overwrites with new data
Slack	Unused space within a cluster
	Attacker may hide malicious code or tools within it
	May contain data from previous files not overwritten by new files

Message Digest and Hash

Maintaining the integrity of a file is extremely important with computer forensics. Hashing can be used to provide proof that data has not been changed. An algorithm applies a mathematical operation to a data stream or file to calculate a unique number based on the information contained in the data stream or file. If someone else takes that file and uses a hash tool, the result will be the same message digest value, if the integrity of the file has been maintained and no modifications have occurred.

Hash should be applied to each file and log:

- Should be written to write-once media

- Provides ability to "bag and tag" evidence

- Proves whether data has been changed or not

Analysis

The steps shown will be taken as in the course of the investigation. Each web browser stores cookies in different places. You can easily find the proper location through research. Tools such as Knoppix Live Linux CD and Helix LiveCD are used to perform computer forensic activities.

Step 1: Check the recycle bin for deleted files.

Step 2: Check the web browser history files.

Step 3: Check the address bar history.

Step 4: Check the web browser cookie files.

Step 5: Check the Temporary Internet Files folders.

Remediation After an Attack

The following are helpful steps to take once an incident has been responded to and the initial investigation completed:

Step 1: Place the system behind a firewall.

Step 2: Reload the OS.

Step 3: Run scanners.

Step 4: Install security software.

Step 5: Remove unneeded services and applications.

Step 6: Apply patches.

Step 7: Restore the system from backup.

Legal Issues

Laws are enacted to enable desired behaviors and prohibit undesired behaviors. Unfortunately, the advancements in information system technologies are much greater than the legal system of compromise and lawmaking. As you continue on in this chapter, you will look at some of the laws and regulations affecting cyberspace. You will have an opportunity to look at several specific laws guiding the policies and procedures developed by an organization to ensure that they are in compliance.

Cybercrime

A computer may be involved in a cybercrime in a couple of different ways. There is computer-assisted crime, computer-targeted crime, and computer-incidental crime. You may be familiar with examples of the first two types of crime. Child pornography provides an example of computer-incidental crime—the computer is used as a storage device and not as an actual tool to enable the crime.

The growth in cybercrime can be attributed to a number of different reasons. There are many tools widely available on the Internet now, and a great deal of expertise is not required to use these tools.

Organizations Created to Fight Cybercrime

There are a number of agencies and organizations out there to aid the fight against cybercrime. It is worthwhile to visit the websites for these organizations to help keep up with the important issues:

- INFRAGARD (`www.infragard.net/`)
- Software & Information Industry Association (`www.siia.net/`)
- National White Collar Crime Center (`www.nw3c.org/`)
- IC3 Internet Crime Complaint Center (`www.ic3.gov/default.aspx`)
- Bureau of Justice Assistance (`www.bja.gov/`)

Sources of Law

In the United States, there are three primary sources of laws and regulations: statutory law, administrative law, and common law. All three sources have an involvement in computer security.

For example, the Computer Fraud and Abuse Act is a statutory law. Administratively, the FCC and Federal Trade Commission have been concerned with issues such as intellectual property theft and fraud. And finally, common law cases work their ways through the judicial system providing precedents and constitutional bases for laws.

Computer Trespass

With the growth of the Internet and global network connections, unauthorized entry into a computer system, or computer trespass, has emerged as a concern that can have national and international consequences. National laws for computer trespass exist in many countries, but there can always be gaps in how these nations handle this type of crime.

Convention of Cybercrime

The Convention on Cybercrime is the first international treaty on Internet crimes (the European Union, the United States, Canada, Japan, and others). Common policies were created to handle cybercrime addressing: copyright infringement, computer-related fraud, child pornography, and violations of network security.

Electronic Communications Privacy Act (ECPA)

The Electronic Communications Privacy Act (ECPA) was passed to address a myriad of legal privacy issues that resulted from the increasing use of computers and other technology specific to telecommunications. Sections of this law address email, cellular communications, workplace privacy, and a host of other issues related to communicating electronically.

Cybercrime and privacy are concepts that are frequently interconnected. A common practice with respect to computer access and privacy today is the use of a warning banner. These banners are typically displayed whenever a network connection occurs and serve four main purposes:

1. From a legal standpoint, the warning banner establishes the level of expected privacy (usually none on a business system).

2. The warning banner serves notice to end users of the intent to conduct real-time monitoring from a business standpoint. Real-time monitoring can be conducted for security reasons, business reasons, or technical network performance reasons.

3. The warning banner obtains the user's consent to monitoring. The key is that the banner tells users that their connection to the network signals their consent to monitoring. Consent can also be obtained to look at files and records. In the case of government systems, consent is needed to prevent direct application of the Fourth Amendment.

4. The warning banner can establish the system or network administrator's common authority to consent to a law enforcement search.

Computer Fraud and Abuse Act (1986)

The Computer Fraud and Abuse Act (CFAA) has been in force for over 20 years and has been amended numerous times. The most recent changes to the law brought about by the USA Patriot Act in 2001 and the Identity Theft Enforcement and Restitution Act in 2008.

The CFAA provides the foundation for US laws criminalizing unauthorized access to computer systems. The CFAA makes it a crime to knowingly access a computer, either considered a government computer or a computer used in interstate commerce, without permission. The CFAA also criminalizes the use of a computer in a crime that is interstate in nature.

The Act criminalizes trafficking in passwords or similar access information. And the act makes it a crime to knowingly transmit a program, code, or command that results in damage.

USA Patriot Act

The Patriot Act changed the level of checks and balances in US law in areas such as Internet wiretaps and tracing and was enacted in response to the terrorist attacks that occurred on September 11, 2001.

One provision of the Patriot Act requires ISPs to cooperate with the federal government and facilitate monitoring of electronic communications on the Internet. Another Provision of the Patriot Act permits federal law enforcement organizations to investigate incidents of computer trespass and enact civil penalties for the perpetrators.

The federal government also amended other computer misuse laws supporting the Patriot Act. Two of these laws were the ECPA and the CFAA which provide multiple tools used by law enforcement to prosecute attackers who trespass systems or use computers to facilitate the theft of information. These laws carry stiff penalties and so are commonly used to convict criminals of computer misuse, even when other charges may have applied.

Gramm–Leach–Bliley Act (GLBA)

The Gramm–Leach–Bliley Act is a piece of legislation that mainly affects the financial industry. A portion of that legislation, though, includes privacy provisions for individuals. The provision provides for opt-out methods so that individuals can control the use of information provided in a business transaction with an organization that is part of the financial institution. The GLBA restricts information sharing with third-party firms and is enforced by state, federal, and securities laws.

Sarbanes–Oxley Act (SOX)

Following several high-profile corporate accounting scandals in the United States, sweeping legislation was passed titled the Sarbanes–Oxley Act (SOX). The purpose of SOX was to overhaul financial and corporate accounting standards and specifically targeted the standards of publicly traded firms in the United States.

Payment Card Industry Data Security Standard (PCI DSS)

Private industry also recognizes how important uniform and enforceable standards are. A Security Standards Council composed of the top corporations in the payment card industry designed a private sector initiative to improve the confidentiality of network communications.

The Payment Card Industry Data Security Standard (PCI DSS) is a set of contractual rules governing how credit card data is to be protected as it is exchanged between merchants and banks. The PCI DSS is a voluntary standard (in theory), and merchants/vendors can choose whether or not they wish to abide by the standard. However, vendor noncompliance may result in significantly higher transaction fees, fines up to $500,000, and possibly even the loss of the ability to process credit cards.

Import/Export Encryption Restrictions

Since World War II, the United States has regulated the export of cryptography due to national security considerations. Nonmilitary cryptography exports are now controlled by the Bureau of Industry and Security in the Department of Commerce. There are still export restrictions to rogue states and terrorist organizations.

Key information regarding United States export control laws

- Administered by the Bureau of Industry and Security

Encryption Rules Can Be Found in Export Administration Regulations (EAR)

Export administration regulations (EAR)[1]

- Includes use to secure network communications.

- Controls include presale product reviews, post-export reporting, and export license reviews.

US Digital Signature Laws

The purpose of the Uniform Electronic Transactions Act is to bring together the differing state laws on issues such as record retention (like checks) and the use of electronic signatures on contracts.

The Electronic Signatures in Global and National Commerce Act facilitates the use of electronic records and electronic signatures in interstate and foreign commerce.

Digital Millennium Copyright Act (DCMA)

The ability of anyone with a PC to make a perfect copy of digital media led to industry fears that individual piracy actions could cause major economic issues in the recording industry. In order to protect the rights of the recording artists and the economic health of the music and movie industry as a whole, the US Congress created the Digital Millennium Copyright Act (DMCA) in 1998. DCMA deals specifically with digital copyright laws in relation to new and ever-advancing technology. A section of the law makes it illegal to develop, produce, and trade any device or mechanism designed to circumvent technological controls used in copy protection.

Privacy

When you take a look at privacy, you are taking a look at the concepts of appropriate use and protection of information. There are many types of privacy. There is personal privacy, informational privacy, and organizational privacy.

Privacy is the ability that you have to keep information about yourself out of the public arena. As you continue this chapter, you will take a look at the laws that have been enacted to protect your privacy in addition to your right to privacy.

---

[1]www.coe.int/en/web/conventions/full-list/-/conventions/treaty/185

Notice, Choice, and Consent

New technologies create new ways to gather information, some of it being private information. The Internet has introduced a whole new set of concerns about privacy. Computers can store everything from photos to public records to your latest status update on Facebook. Many employers will do online research on a candidate before hiring that individual.

Many online transactions require personally identifiable information (PII). PII can be used to identify a specific individual, even if all of the information is not disclosed. Privacy policies govern organizations that collect PII. You should be familiar with all three terms to ensure that your PII is not being used in a way that you did not intend.

- **Notice** refers to informing the customer that personally identifying information (PII) will be collected and used and/or stored.

- **Choice** refers to the opportunity for the end user to consent to the data collection or to opt out.

- **Consent** refers to the positive affirmation by a customer that he or she read the notice, understands his or her choices, and in turn has agreed to release his or her PII for the purposes explained.

US Privacy Laws

All of the laws listed here include a provision for dealing with privacy. Please review the US Privacy Laws for specific details regarding each of the following laws:

- Privacy Act of 1974

- Freedom of Information ACT (FOIA)

- Family Education Records and Privacy Act (FERPA)

- US Computer Fraud and Abuse Act (CFAA)

- US Children's Online Privacy Protection Act (COPPA)

- Video Privacy Protection Act (VPPA)

- Health Insurance Portability and Accountability Act

- Gramm–Leach–Bliley Act (GLBA)

- California Senate Bill 1386 (SB 1386)

- US Banking Rules and Regulations

- Payment Card Industry Data Security Standard (PCI DSS)

- Fair Credit Reporting Act (FCRA)

Privacy Policies

Policies are the best way to ensure compliance across an organization, and a privacy policy plays an important role within the organization, especially with the numerous laws enacted to protect privacy. One of the direct outcomes of the legal statutes associated with privacy has been the development of a need for corporate privacy policies associated with data collection.

Privacy Impact Assessment (PIA)

A privacy impact assessment can be conducted to ensure that personally identifiable information (PII) is properly handled throughout an organization.

1. Establish PIA scope.

2. Identify key stakeholders.

3. Document all contact with PII.

4. Review legal and regulatory requirements.

5. Document gaps and potential issues between requirements and practices.

6. Review findings with key stakeholders.

Summary

In this chapter you learned about multiple response procedures and methods for how to deal with incidents. You reviewed concepts relating to computer forensics, the incident response model, and the basics of how to procure evidence. In this chapter you also had the opportunity to learn about laws which guide the policies and procedures used to ensure compliance.

Resources

- **INFRAGARD**: www.infragard.net/

- **Software & Information Industry Association**: www.siia.net/

- **National White Collar Crime Center**: www.nw3c.org/

- **IC3 Internet Crime Complaint Center**: www.ic3.gov/default.aspx

- **Bureau of Justice Assistance**: www.bja.gov/

- **Convention on Cybercrime**: www.coe.int/en/web/conventions/full-list/-/conventions/treaty/185

- **Export Administration Regulations**: www.bis.doc.gov/index.php/regulations/export-administration-regulations-ear

CHAPTER 9

Attacks

Attacks are possible at many levels, from network protocols to applications. The effects of an attack can vary from minor to severe. In this chapter, you will learn about the steps that an attacker can take. By understanding these steps, you can better limit the exposure of your system. Many attacks exploit known vulnerabilities for which there are patches.

By the end of this chapter, you will be able to

1. Identify the different types of malware that exist.

2. Describe computer attacks.

Avenue of Attacks

Generally, computer systems are attacked either as specific targets or merely as targets of opportunity. An attacker's motivation in specifically targeting a system may be political, monetary, or other. In these instances, the choice to attack does not rely on the exact hardware and software being used in the targeted system but rather proceeds in spite of these details. Target of opportunity attacks succeed when systems are found which have not been updated with the most current security patches and are therefore vulnerable to specific exploits. See Figure 9-1.

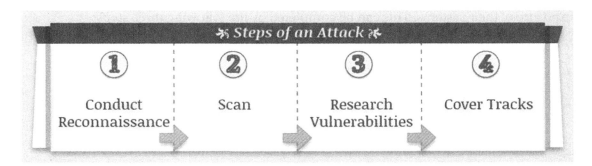

Figure 9-1. *Steps of an Attack*

© Ahmed F. Sheikh 2020
A. F Sheikh, *CompTIA Security+ Certification Study Guide*, https://doi.org/10.1007/978-1-4842-6234-4_9

1. **Conduct Reconnaissance**: The first step of an attack is to gather as much information as possible about the system or organization being targeted. Key data would include names, phone numbers, IP addresses, networks maintained by the organization, and even the organizational structure or hierarchy. This information can be gathered through open source Internet searches of web pages and FTP sites through Google or another search engine. Information can also be acquired using resources such as the SEC's EDGAR website[1] which provides numerous financial reports. Additional information can be gathered using tools such as Whois.Net[2] to link registrants and IP addresses.

2. **Scan**: It is not always clear as to what information will be needed to make the attack successful. That is why an attacker will gather as much as can be found using as many sources as possible. During the scan phase, there may be a ping sweep, port scan, or an analysis on packet response.

3. **Research Vulnerabilities**: As the attack moves forward through the scanning and vulnerability research phase, some of the information may prove more valuable than originally thought. Once vulnerabilities are researched and determinations are made, the *attack is matched to the identified vulnerability*, and *a backdoor is created*.

4. **Cover Tracks**: Finally, tracks are then covered by erasing pertinent files and changing file time stamps.

Minimizing Possible Avenues of Attack

In order to minimize the possibility of an attack, an administrator should limit the exposure of their systems. This can be completed by the following three steps:

1. Ensure all patches are installed and up to date.

2. Limit the services being run on the system.

3. Limit the amount of publicly available data about the system and organization.

---

[1]www.sec.gov/edgar.shtml
[2]www.whois.net/

Attacking Computer Systems and Networks

An attack can be defined as an attempt by an unauthorized individual to gain access to or modify information without proper permission, assume control of an authorized session, or disrupt the availability of a service or system resources to authorized users. Attacks on specific software rely on code flaws or software bugs and indicate lack of thorough code testing. Attacks on specific protocol or service take advantage of or use a service or protocol in an unintended manner.

Phishing and Pharming

Phishing and pharming are two tools used for identity theft and are common attack methods used to steal credentials. See Figure 9-2.

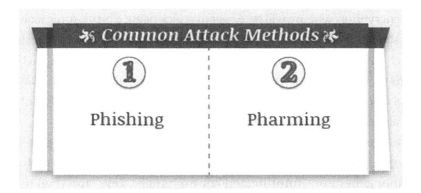

Figure 9-2. *Common Attack Methods*

1. **Phishing** is the use of fraudulent emails or instant messages that appear to be genuine but are designed to trick users. The goal of a phishing attack is to obtain from the user information that can be used in an attack, such as log-in credentials or other critical information. When the attacker includes information that should be known only to the entity that they are impersonating, the attack is called spear phishing.

2. **Pharming** is the impersonation of a website in an effort to deceive a user into entering their credentials. The Anti-Phishing Working Group (APWG) is an industry association focused on eliminating the identity theft and fraud that result from phishing and email spoofing.

Attacks on Encryption

Cryptographic systems can be compromised in various ways. Certain encryption algorithms may have specific keys that yield poor or easily decrypted ciphertext. Some algorithms have been found to have weak keys that make cryptanalysis easier.

Even if the specific algorithm used to encrypt a message is complicated and has not been shown to have weak keys, the key length will still play a significant role in how easy it is to attack the method of encryption. Generally speaking, the longer a key, the harder it will be to attack. Thus, a 40-bit encryption scheme will be easier to attack using a brute-force technique than a 256-bit-based scheme. The strength of the encryption method is related to the sheer size of the keyspace, which with modern algorithms is large enough to provide significant time constraints when using this method to break an encrypted message. Algorithmic complexity is also an issue with respect to brute force, and you cannot immediately compare different key lengths from different algorithms and assume relative strength.

One of the most common ways of attacking an encryption system is to find weaknesses in mechanisms surrounding the cryptography. Examples include poor random-number generators, unprotected key exchanges, keys stored on hard drives without sufficient protection, and other general programmatic errors. In attacks that target these types of weaknesses, it is not the cryptographic algorithm itself that is being attacked but rather the implementation of that algorithm in the real world.

Password Attacks

The combination of a user ID and a password is the most common form of system authentication. When this combination fails, it is typically the result of users failing to adhere to good password procedures. Some password attack methods include the following types of information, approaches, or efforts: birthday, hybrid, brute force, dictionary, and guessing.

Injection Attacks

An injection attack is a technique that exploits a vulnerability in an application's software. Malicious code is inserted into strings that are later passed to an SQL server for processing. Injection attacks can be used to attack a website or any type of SQL database. A result of an injection attack can be that the attacker gets a dump of the database contents.

Types of injection attacks

- SQL injection

- Command injection

- LDAP injection

- XML injection

Software Exploitation

Software exploitation encompasses attacks which take advantage of software bugs or weaknesses. These bugs and weaknesses may be the result of poor design, inadequate testing, or inferior coding practices. They may also come from additional features built into the program to assist in development and then forgotten.

One example of software being exploited is a buffer overflow attack where a program receives more input data than it is designed to handle. Historically, buffer overflows have been one of the most common software vulnerabilities.

Improperly configured programs cannot handle the buffer overflow, and the extra characters continue to fill memory and eventually begin to overwrite other portions of the program. A buffer overflow can cause a program to abort, cause the entire system to crash, or even allow an attacker to execute a command within the program.

Malicious Code

Malicious code is a term used to describe software that was designed to disrupt computer operation or gain access to computer systems without the user's knowledge or permission. Malware includes a variety of malicious programs each differentiated by their own characteristics as defined in Figure 9-3. The majority of malware threats are worms or Trojans.

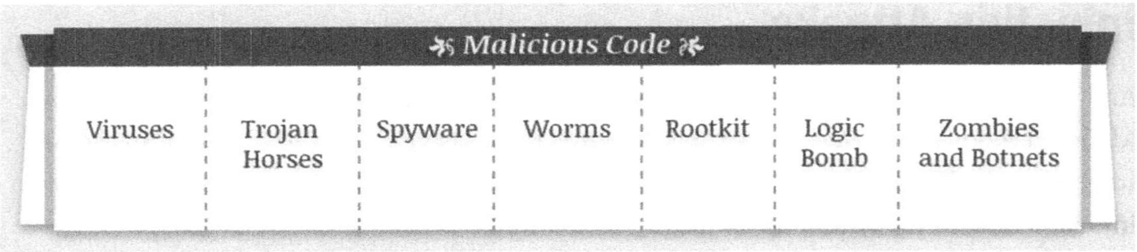

Figure 9-3. *Malicious Code Types*

1. **Viruses** require a host.

2. **Trojan horses** are legitimate-looking stand-alone programs installed by a user.

3. **Spyware** is typically installed unbeknownst to users and is used to monitor software and system use.

4. **Worms** are code that penetrate and replicate on a system.

5. **Rootkits** modify the OS kernel or other processes on a system.

6. **Logic bombs** are triggered by an event.

7. **Zombies** and **Botnets** are malware installed on machines which create armies.

Malware Defense

Attacks against a system can occur at the network level, operating system level, application level, or user level (like social engineering).

Early malware attack patterns targeted networks, but most of today's sophisticated malware attacks target a combination of network, OS, and application vulnerabilities.

There are a few simple steps that when applied can defend against all forms of malware. See Figure 9-4.

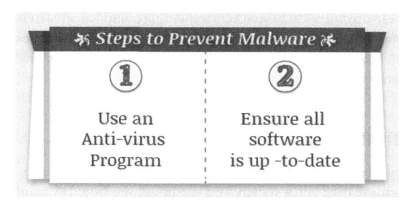

Figure 9-4. *Steps to Prevent Malware*

1. **Antivirus Program**: Use an effective antivirus program. The majority of antivirus suites are designed to catch most widespread forms of malware. However, there are many new threats being developed and deployed on a daily basis. Therefore, the key to an effective antivirus solution is to keep the signatures updated.

2. **Up-to-Date Software**: Ensure all software is up to date to avoid malware. Many forms of malware achieve their objectives through exploitation of vulnerabilities in software, both in the operating system and applications. Although operating system vulnerabilities were the main source of problems, today's application-level vulnerabilities pose the greatest risk. The majority of attacks that occur happen within the application level where the target data resides. Unfortunately, while operating system vendors are becoming more and more responsive to patching, most application vendors are not.

War-Dialing and War-Driving

War-dialing is an attempt by an attacker to find unprotected modem connections to an organization's computer systems and networks. Success is often the result of authorized individuals connecting unauthorized or rogue modems to the network. The authorized user's intent is not usually malicious, but the results can be. In recent years, advances in telephone firewalls have severely restricted unauthorized connections while also increasing the security of authorized modems as well.

The term war-driving refers to attackers wandering around an area (often in a car), searching for available wireless network connections. There are security measures built into both the hardware and software tasked with maintaining a wireless access point, but it will only operate as well as it is configured.

Social Engineering

Sometimes attackers prefer to gain information through people rather than by using a technical means to hack into a system. This can be accomplished by manipulating authorized users into providing access or divulging confidential information to an attacker through lies or misrepresentation.

Social engineering can apply to efforts to gain either virtual or physical access to a system. The following scenario provided is a common example of how individuals are manipulated into providing access to an attacker.

Scenario

Jim: Hi, Bob. This is Jim from ABC, your ISP. Your Internet connection is presenting a problem. Can I get your password so that I can fix it?

Bob: Oh my gosh. Am I going to lose service? Jim, my password is b0bSm1th.

Security Auditing

Audits are the method used to assess the overall security of an organization in comparison to an established standard. Audits also measure how effective deployed countermeasures actually are in mitigating previously identified risks.

Security audits should be conducted on a regular basis and may be mandated depending on the industry. In a lot of instances, they can be contracted out to another party. The focus of a security audit should be on the security perimeter of the organization and the system; all of an organization's policies, procedures, and guidelines governing security; and the training of all employees that will be involved with the system.

Summary

In this chapter you learned about the various types of malware and approaches that a potential attacker may take against network protocols or applications. You also reviewed how to minimize possible avenues of attack by implementing safeguards.

Resources

- **SEC's EDGAR**: www.sec.gov/edgar.shtml
- **Whois.Net**: www.whois.net/

CHAPTER 10

Network Attacks

In this chapter, you will learn about the various threats that an attacker can launch against a network. Attacks on a specific protocol or service are attempts to take advantage of a specific feature or to use the protocol or service in a way that was not intended. You will gain an understanding of different types of network attacks and how to use assessment tools to help determine security.

By the end of this chapter, you will be able to

1. Analyze and differentiate among types of network attacks.

2. Analyze and differentiate among types of wireless attacks.

Denial-of-Service Attack

The goal of a denial-of-service, or DoS, attack is to deny access to authorized users making the network unavailable (remember the three underlying security principles, confidentiality, integrity, and availability). A distributed denial-of-service, or DDoS, attack uses many zombies, or soldier attackers, to overwhelm a target. See Figure 10-1. To prevent DoS and DDoS attacks, ensure patches and upgrades are current, change time-out period for TCP connections, distribute the workload across server systems, and block external ICMP packets at the border. Recall that command line commands such as ping use ICMP packets.

© Ahmed F. Sheikh 2020
A. F Sheikh, *CompTIA Security+ Certification Study Guide*, https://doi.org/10.1007/978-1-4842-6234-4_10

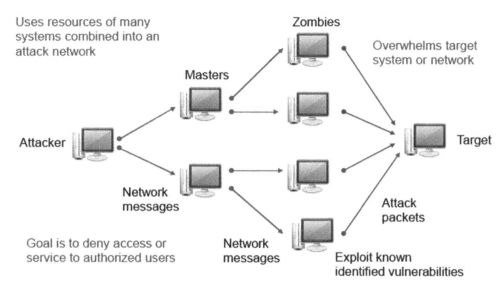

Figure 10-1. *Denial of Service Attack*

Three-Way Handshake

You should have a basic understanding of the three-way handshake that the TCP/IP protocol uses to establish a connection. First, System 1 sends a SYN packet to System 2 indicating a desire to communicate with the system. Then, System 2 responds to System 1 by sending back the SYN packet combined with an ACK packet to indicate its willingness to accept communications. Once System 1 receives the SYN/ACK packet, it responds with an ACK packet, and communications are then established between the systems. Please see Figure 10-2.

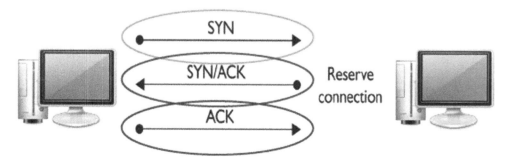

Figure 10-2. *A Three-Way Handshake Process*

SYN Flood Attack

A SYN flood attack takes advantage of the three-way handshake by overwhelming the target with SYN requests to a bogus server. If the attack can outpace the requests' timing out, the target will be in limbo waiting for system responses that do not exist. For instance

1. Communication request sent to target system using a fake IP address. Note that if the attacks outpace the requests timing out, then system's resources will be exhausted.

2. Target responds to fake IP address.

3. Target waits for nonexistent system response.

4. Request eventually times out.

See Figure 10-3 for an example.

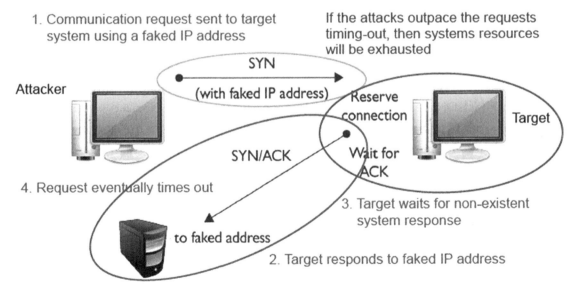

Figure 10-3. *SYN Flood Attack Using a Three-Way Handshake*

Ping of Death (POD)

A Ping-of-Death attack is an example of a DoS attack which targets a specific protocol or operating system. The attacker sends an Internet Control Message Protocol (ICMP) ping packet equal to or greater than 64KB. This type of packet should not occur naturally. Some systems cannot handle the packet and will hang or crash.

Trapdoors and Backdoors

Originally, backdoors referred to efforts by software developers to ensure access to a program that bypassed the normal access methods. Over time, this practice has come to be known as creating a trapdoor into a program. One problem with a trapdoor is that since it is hard-coded into the program, it can be very difficult, if not impossible, to remove. A benefit to software developers and system administrators in using a trapdoor is that it ensures access to a program even if the normal access methods fail. However, this benefit is now a vulnerability. The trapdoor offers full access into the system where an attacker could cause serious harm.

More recently, a backdoor has come to refer to the programs or code introduced by an attacker that has compromised a system. A few common backdoor programs are Netbus and Back Orifice which both allow remote access to unauthorized system users. The purpose of the backdoor is to grant the attacker future access to the system even if the original vulnerability used to attack the system has been fixed. Usually, backdoors are installed on systems by unauthorized users or attackers. However, they can also be installed by authorized users who inadvertently run a Trojan horse program on their machine which then installs the backdoor.

Similar to the backdoor, another method employed by attackers is to install a rootkit on a system that ensures continued root access for the attacker.

Null Sessions

A null session is a connection to a Windows inter-process communication share (IPC$). A vulnerability exists in Microsoft Windows systems prior to the XP and Server 2003 versions of the operating system. The Server Message Block (SMB) system allows users to establish a null session. A wide range of tools and malware use this vulnerability to achieve their aim.

One way to defend against the creation of null sessions is to upgrade the systems to Windows XP, Server 2003, or newer version. You can also limit TCP ports 139 and 445 to only allow trusted user access.

Sniffing

Sniffing occurs when an attacker examines all network traffic as it passes their NIC independent of whether or not the traffic is addressed to them or not. Network sniffing can be accomplished with a software application, hardware device, or a combination of the two. Sniffing can be used to view all network traffic, or it can target a specific protocol, service, or even string of characters such as a log-in or password. Some network sniffers are designed not just to observe all traffic but to modify some or all of the traffic as well. Network administrators may also use sniffers to analyze network traffic, identify bandwidth issues, and troubleshoot other network issues. Physical security is important in preventing the introduction of sniffers on the internal network.

IP Address Spoofing

In a specific DoS attack known as a smurf attack, the attacker sends a spoofed packet to the broadcast address for a network, which distributes the packet to all systems on that network. In the smurf attack, the packet sent by the attacker to the broadcast address is an echo request with the **From** address forged so that it appears that another system (the target system) has made the echo request.

The normal response of a system to an echo request is an echo reply, and it is used in the ping utility to let a user know whether a remote system is reachable and is responding. Should the attacker send several of these spoofed requests, or send them to several different networks, the target can quickly become overwhelmed with the volume of echo replies it receives. See Figure 10-4.

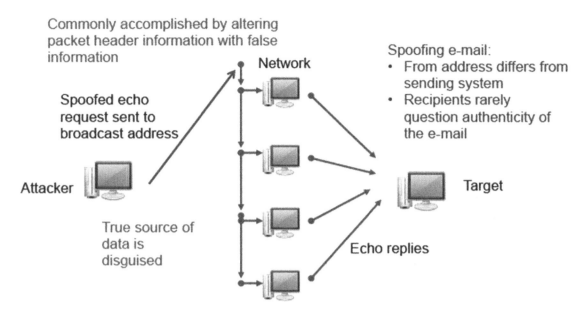

Figure 10-4. *ID Address Spoofing*

Spoofing and Trusted Relationships

Spoofing can also take advantage of a trusted relationship between two systems.

If two systems are configured to accept the authentication accomplished by each other, an individual logged onto one system might not be forced to go through an authentication process again to access the other system. An attacker can take advantage of this arrangement by sending a packet to one system that appears to have come from a trusted system. Since the trusted relationship is in place, the targeted system may perform the requested task without authentication.

Since a reply will often be sent once a packet is received, the system that is being impersonated could interfere with the attack, since it would receive an acknowledgement for a request it never made. The attacker will often initially launch a disk operating system (DoS) attack (such as a SYN flooding attack) to temporarily take out the spoofed system for the period of time that the attacker is exploiting the trusted relationship.

Once the attack is completed, the DoS attack on the spoofed system would be terminated, and the system administrator might never notice that the attack occurred. See Figure 10-5.

Firewalls should also be configured to discard any packets from outside of the firewall that have From addresses indicating they originated from inside the network. This is a situation that should not occur normally, and it indicates spoofing is being attempted.

The attacker launches a SYN flooding attack to temporarily take out the spoofed system for the period of time that the attacker is exploiting the trusted relationship

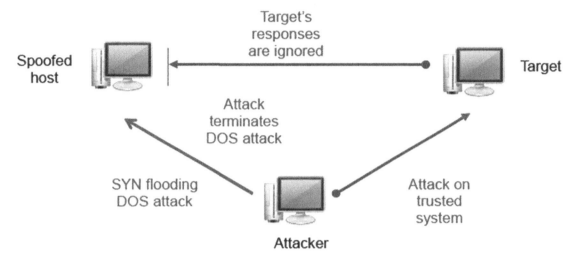

Figure 10-5. *An SYN Flooding Attack*

Spoofing and Sequence Numbers

In the transmission control protocol (TCP) three-way handshake, two sets of sequence numbers are created. The first system chooses a sequence number to send with the original SYN packet. When the second host responds and sends its own SYN packet, it generates another sequence number.

The second host also sends an ACK packet in response to the first host's SYN packet. The ACK packet includes the original sequence number incremented by 1. The original host system receives the SYN/ACK with both sequence numbers and then increments the second host's sequence number by one and passes it back in an ACK packet response.

Spoofing attacks from inside a network are typically easier than attacks from outside a network because an attacker can more easily observe the traffic inside the network and can do a better job of formulating the necessary packets. If the attacker is inside the network and can observe the traffic with which a target host responds, the attacker can easily see the sequence number the system creates and can respond with the correct sequence number. If the attacker is external to the network and the sequence number the target system generates is not observed, it is next to impossible for the attacker to provide the final ACK with the correct sequence number. See Figure 10-6.

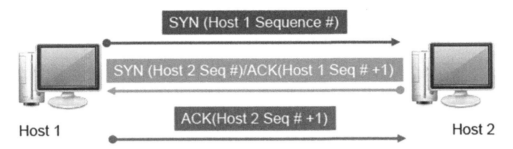

Figure 10-6. *Spoofing and Sequence Process*

Man-in-the-Middle Attack

When an attacker successfully inserts themselves between two other hosts' communications by spoofing addresses, it is referred to as a man-in-the-middle attack. A man-in-the-middle attack is usually accomplished by manipulating a router to alter the path of the traffic. The traffic is sent to the attacker rather than the intended target and then relayed onto the target host. This enables the attacker to observe the traffic from each target host in route and may even allow the attacker to modify or block certain messages. Since all expected replies are received by the target hosts, it can appear to them that communications are occurring normally. If the data being intercepted from the target hosts is encrypted, the attacker may only be able to get a limited amount of information. Review Figure 10-7 for an illustration of a man-in-the-middle Attack as described in this section.

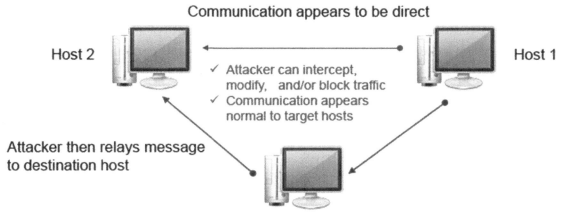

Figure 10-7. *Illustration of Man-in-the-Middle Attack*

Replay Attack

A replay attack occurs when an attacker captures a portion of a communication between two hosts and then retransmits the captured message at a later time. Replay attacks are often used to circumvent authentication mechanisms. Systems can prevent falling victim to a replay attack by encrypting traffic, providing cryptographic authentication, and including a time stamp with each portion of the message. For illustration see Figure 10-8.

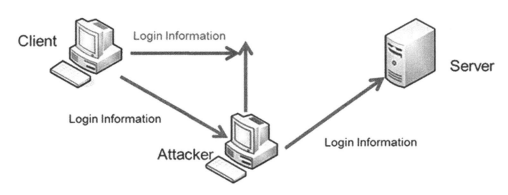

Figure 10-8. *Replay Attack*

TCP/IP Hijacking

Transmission Control Protocol/Internet Protocol (TCP/IP) hijacking and session hijacking are terms used to refer to the process of taking control of an already existing session between a client and a server. The advantage to an attacker of hijacking over attempting to penetrate a computer system or network is that the attacker does not have to circumvent any authentication mechanisms.

To prevent the user from noticing anything unusual, the attacker may target the user's system with a DoS attack, taking it down so that the user, and the system, will not notice the extra traffic that is taking place.

Hijack attacks generally are used against web and Telnet sessions. Refer to Figure 10-9 for an example of TCP/IP hijacking.

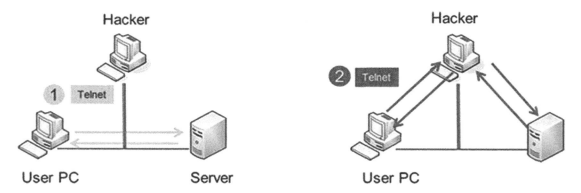

Figure 10-9. *TCP/IP Hijacking*

Drive-By Download Attack

A drive-by download attack is accomplished by initiating downloads of malware, whether a user clicks it or not. Drive-by downloads can initiate from a couple of different mechanisms. It is possible for an ad that is rotated into content on a reputable site to contain a drive-by download. Users do not have control over what ads are presented. A second, more common method is a website that the user gets to either by mistyping a URL or by following a search link without being sure of what they are clicking for. Review Figure 10-10 for an illustration.

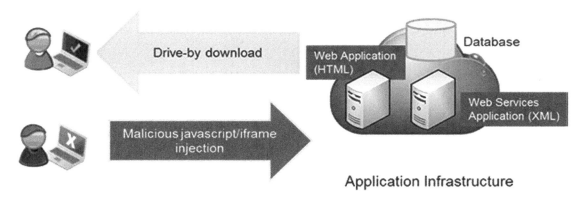

Figure 10-10. *Drive-By Download Attack*

Summary

It is important to be aware of the various types of potential threats that an attacker may launch against a network. In this chapter you learned about different types of network attacks and the use of assessment tools that can be applied to determine security threats and vulnerabilities to safeguard against attacks.

CHAPTER 11

Baseline and Secure Software Development

To secure a system effectively, you need to take a structured approach. You must fully understand the intended function of the system. What applications are required? What processes and services are needed? Regardless of the type of software, there is a universal requirement that the software performs the desired functions and performs them in the correct manner. Developers know that functional specifications must be met for the software to be satisfactory. As we depend more and more on computers driven by software, we will need systems to do the same—to not only function now but to be protected from malfunction in the future. In this chapter you will learn about the importance of application and data security and procedures required for host security.

By the end of this chapter, you will be able to

1. Explain the importance of application security.

2. Carry out appropriate procedures to establish host security.

3. Explain the importance of data security.

Overview of Baselines

The process of establishing a system's security state is called **baselining**. To harden a system, we will start with an examination of the system's intended functions and capabilities to determine what processes and applications will be housed on the system. As a best practice, anything that is not required for operation should be removed or disabled on the system. Apply all of the appropriate patches, hotfixes, and settings to protect it.

© Ahmed F. Sheikh 2020
A. F Sheikh, *CompTIA Security+ Certification Study Guide*, https://doi.org/10.1007/978-1-4842-6234-4_11

Uniform baselines are critical in a large-scale environment, because maintaining separate configurations and security levels for hundreds of systems or more is far too costly. Additionally, similar systems can be configured with the same baseline to achieve the same level of security and protection.

Operating System and Network/Operating System Hardening

The process of securing and preparing a system for the production environment is called **hardening**. The operating system of a computer is the basic software that handles things such as input, output, display, memory management, and all the other tasks required to support the user environment and associated applications. A network operating system (NOS) is an operating system that includes additional functions and capabilities to assist in connecting computers and devices, such as printers, to a local area network (LAN). See Figure 11-1.

Consider the following actions:

- Disabling unnecessary services

- Restricting permissions on files and directories

- Removing unnecessary software

- Applying patches

- Removing unnecessary users

- Applying password guidelines

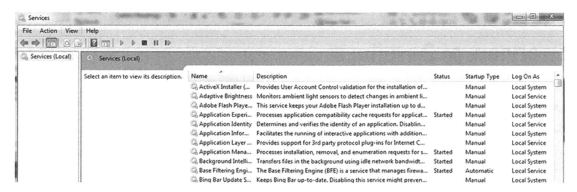

Figure 11-1. *Windows Operating System Services Screen Which Includes a View of the Name, Description, Status, Startup Type, and Log-On As Information*

Hardening Windows

It is important to be aware of how to address hardening the Windows operating system. Several specific suggestions are discussed and provided here:

1. The user account used day to day should not be a member of the Administrators local group.

2. Change the network type to Public:

   • Network discovery disabled

   • File and Printer Sharing disabled

3. Configure the Windows Firewall.

   • Drop all inbound connections automatically so that no one will be able to access anything on the computer from the network.

   • Filter outgoing traffic and applications to protect personal files.

4. Change the User Account Settings to the highest level.

5. Configure Data Execution Prevention (DEP) to monitor programs to make sure they use computer memory safely.

   • Go to System ➤ Advanced System Settings ➤ Performance ➤ Settings ➤ Data Execution Prevention: Set to All Programs (set exceptions)

6. Disable remote assistance and remote desktop connections.

7. Disable sharing and the NetBIOS protocol to completely remove the option to share files.

8. Disable unnecessary services:

   • TCP/IP NetBIOS helper

   • Server Service

   • Computer browser

   • Remote Registry

   • HomeGroup Listener

   • HomeGroup Provider

See Figure 11-2 for an example of a User Account Control window which advises that Windows needs your permission to continue. You will need to select the Continue button to change computer settings. Remember that User Account Controls can be used to eliminate unauthorized changes to your computer.

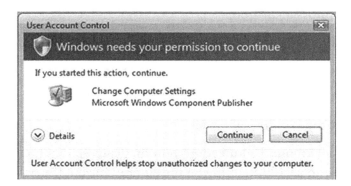

Figure 11-2. *Windows Operating System Services User Account Control Window*

Hardening Windows 2019 Server

Microsoft has a free hardening guide for the 2019 OS available from its Download Center.

- Network Access Protection (NAP) controls access to network resources based on a client computer's identity and compliance with corporate governance policy. NAP allows network administrators to define granular levels of network access based on client identity, group membership, and the degree to which that client is compliant with corporate policies. See Figure 11-3.

- Read-only domain controllers can be created and deployed in high-risk locations, but they can't be modified to add new users, change access levels, and so on.

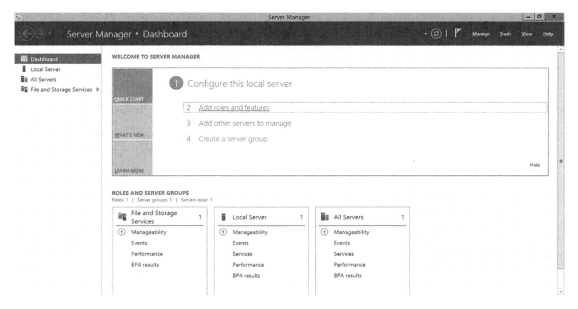

Figure 11-3. *Windows OS Initial Configuration Tasks Screen*

Hardening UNIX- or Linux-Based Operating Systems

Most organizations do not use a UNIX or Linux system as a desktop alternative for users. In most cases, these machines will be servers with very specific functions. During the initial installation, software or other services may be installed by default to make the installation go smoothly for the average user. Since the defaults may be unnecessary to the function of the server, the software should be removed, and the unnecessary services should be disabled. See Figure 11-4.

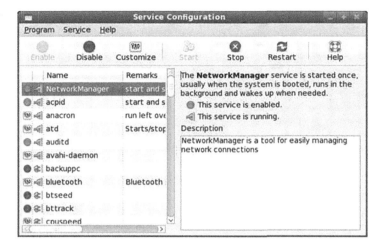

Figure 11-4. *Service Configuration Window*

Hardening Linux: Managing User Accounts

The root account has complete and total control over the system and should therefore be protected with an exceptionally strong password. Many administrators will configure their systems to prevent anyone from logging in directly as root. Instead, they must log in with their own personal accounts and switch to the root account using the **su** command.

Adding user accounts can be done with the **useradd** command, and unwanted user accounts can be removed using the **userdel** command. Additionally, you can manually edit/etc/passwd to add or remove user accounts.

User accounts can also be managed via a graphic user interface (GUI). See Figure 11-5.

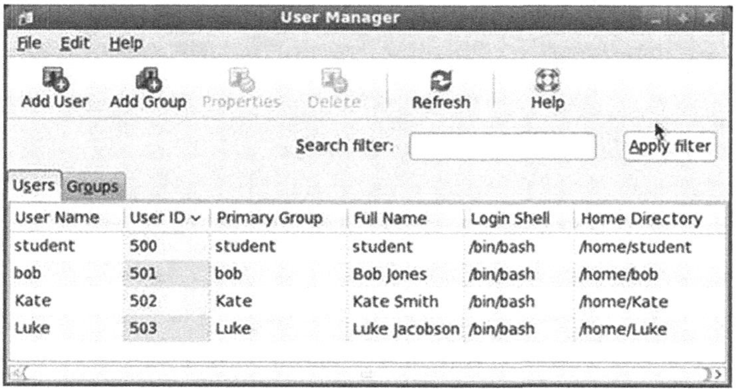

Figure 11-5. *User Manager Screen Reflecting the User Name, User ID, Primary Group, Full Name, Login Shell, and Home Directory*

Hardening Linux: Firewall Configuration

Administrators may choose a security level, from high, medium, off, to a customized option that enables them to individually select which ports on which interfaces external users may connect to. In addition to the built-in firewall functions, administrators may also use TCP wrappers.

By specifying host and port combinations in /etc/hosts.allow, administrators can allow certain hosts to connect on certain ports. The firewall function and hosts.allow must work together if both functions are used on the same system. The connection must be allowed by both utilities, or it will be dropped. See Figure 11-6.

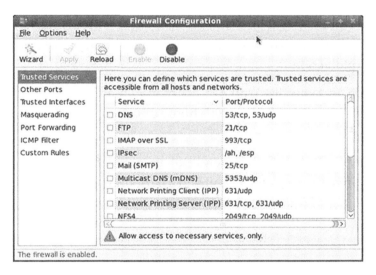

Figure 11-6. *Firewall Configuration Screen*

Hardening Mac OS X

In the Mac OS X 10.15 (Catalina) release, Apple included some new security-specific features to help protect its user base:

- Only processes that are explicitly granted access are allowed to access system resources such as networking, file systems, process execution, and so on.

- Any file downloaded with Safari, iChat, or Mail is automatically tagged with metadata, including the source URL, date and time of download, and so on. If the download was an archive (such as a zip file), the same metadata is tagged to any file extracted from the archive. Users are prompted with this information the first time they try to run or open the downloaded file.

- Catalina provides no execution stack protection. Essentially, this means that certain portions of the stack have been marked as "data only," and the OS will not execute any instructions in regions marked as data only. This helps protect against buffer overflow attacks.

- Catalina loads system libraries into random locations, making it harder for attackers to reference static system library locations in their exploit code.

- FileVault encrypts files with AES encryption. When this feature is enabled, everything in the user's home directory is automatically encrypted.

- The new Apple Application firewall allows users to restrict network access on both a per-application and a per-port basis. See Figure 11-7.

Figure 11-7. *Mac OS X 10.15: Security Window*

Hardening Mac OS X: File Permissions

Traditionally, the Mac OS was largely ignored by the hacker community. With the rise in the number of Macs on the market, Mac users should anticipate a sharp increase in unwanted attention and scrutiny from potential attackers. See Figure 11-8.

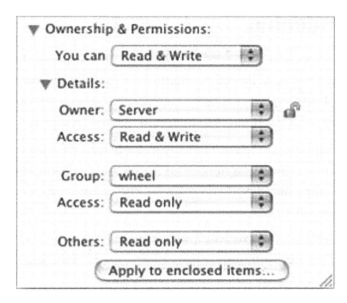

Figure 11-8. *Mac OS Ownership and Permissions Window*

Updates

Vendors typically follow a hierarchy for software updates. Three types of updates are listed here:

- **Hotfix**: The hotfix is usually a small software update designed to address a specific problem, such as a buffer overflow in an application that exposes the system to attacks. Hotfixes are typically developed in reaction to a discovered problem and are produced and then released rather quickly. Hotfixes typically address critical, security-related issues and should be applied to the affected application or operating system as soon as possible.

- **Patch**: Patches are usually applied as a more formal, larger software update that may address several software problems. Patches often contain enhancements or additional capabilities as well as fixes for known bugs and are usually developed over a longer period of time.

- **Service Pack**: A service pack is a large collection of patches and hotfixes rolled into a single package. Service packs are designed to bring a system up to the latest known, good level all at once, rather than requiring the user or system administrator to download dozens or hundreds of updates separately.

Network Hardening

The same logical approach to hardening a system can also be applied to hardening a network. Software updates and device configurations for each network component must be addressed. Ports support various network services. Network devices must be configured with very strict parameters to maintain network security.

- Software updates maintain current vendor patch levels for your infrastructure. The different vendors for the different software and hardware must be tracked and software and firmware for each device must be kept current.

- Device configuration involves limiting access, choosing good passwords, turning off unnecessary services, and changing SNMP community strings.

Application Hardening

Application hardening secures an application against local and Internet-based attacks. Most users are much more diligent about keeping their operating systems updated with the latest patches, but applications should also be a concern. Patch management is a disciplined approach to the acquisition, testing, and implementation of patches.

1. **Application Patches**: Include hotfixes, patches, and upgrades.

2. **Patch Management**: Microsoft provides a free patch management product at the Microsoft site called Windows Server Update Services (WSUS). Using the WSUS product, administrators can manage updates for any compatible Windows-based system in their organization. The WSUS product can be configured to download patches automatically from Microsoft based on a variety of factors (such as OS, product family, criticality, and so on). When updates are downloaded, the administrator can determine whether or not to push out the patches and when to apply them to the systems in their environment. The WSUS product can also help administrators track patch status on their systems, which is a useful and necessary feature.

Patch management involves the notification of patches, continual scanning of systems patch status, selection of which patches to apply, pushing patches to systems, the ability to report a patch success or failure, and the ability to report patch status on any or all systems in the environment. See Figure 11-9.

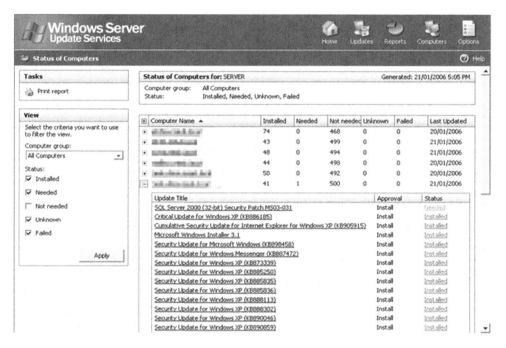

Figure 11-9. *Microsoft Window Server Update Services*

Group Policies

Group policies allow for centralized management and configuration of computers and remote users in an Active Directory environment. See Figure 11-10. Policy settings are stored in a group policy object (GPO) and are referenced internally by the OS using a globally unique identifier (GUID).

Group policy capabilities

- Network location awareness can apply different GPOs as needed.

- Mobile users who connect through VPNs can receive a GPO update in the background after connecting to the corporate network via VPN.

- Power management can be managed.

- Administrators can restrict user access to USB drives, CD-RW drives, DVD-RW drives, and other removable media.

- Users can be assigned to various printers based on their location. As mobile users move, their printer locations can be updated to the closest local printer.

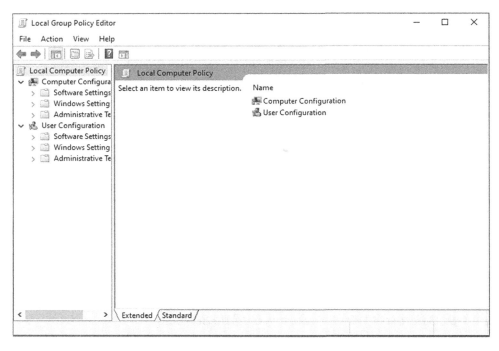

Figure 11-10. *Windows OS Group Policy Object Editor Screen*

Security Templates

A security template is simply a collection of security settings that can be applied to a system. Within the Windows OS, security templates can contain hundreds of settings that control or modify system settings such as password length, auditing of user actions, or restrictions on network access. Security templates can be stand-alone files that are applied manually to each system, but they can also be part of a group policy, allowing common security settings to be applied to systems on a much wider scale. See Figure 11-11.

Here is a collection of security settings that can be applied to a system:

- **Account policies** are settings for user accounts, such as password length, complexity requirements, and account lockouts.

- **Event log settings** apply to the three main audit logs within Windows (Application, System, and Security), such as log file size and retention of older entries.

- **File permissions** apply to files and folders, such as permission inheritance and locking permissions.

- **Registry permissions** control who can access the Registry and how it can be accessed.

- **System services** are settings for services that run on the system, such as startup mode and whether or not users can stop/start a service.

- **User rights** control what a user can and cannot do on the system.

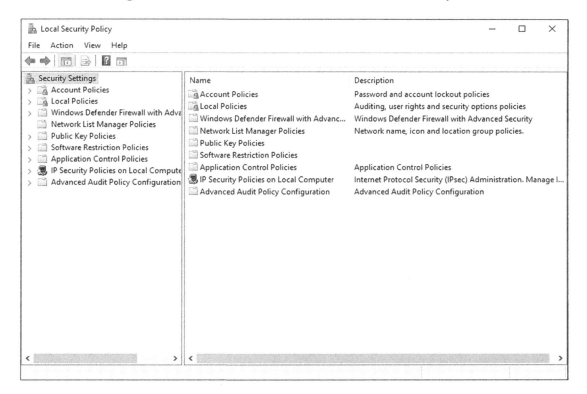

Figure 11-11. *Windows OS Local Security Policy Window Showing the Security Templates Available*

Secure Software Development

Regardless of the type of software, there is a universal requirement that the software performs the desired functions and performs them in the correct manner. Developers know that functional specifications must be met for the software to be satisfactory.

As we depend more and more on computers driven by software, we will need systems to do the same—to not only function now but to be protected from malfunction in the future.

Software Engineering

Software engineering fits as many requirements as possible into the project management schedule timeline. But with analysts and developers working with abbreviated timelines to get as many functional elements correct as possible, the issue of nonfunctional requirements often gets pushed to the back burner or neglected entirely.

Getting security right in a program is essential if we are going to rely on a program. Security is best if built into the foundation. See Figure 11-12.

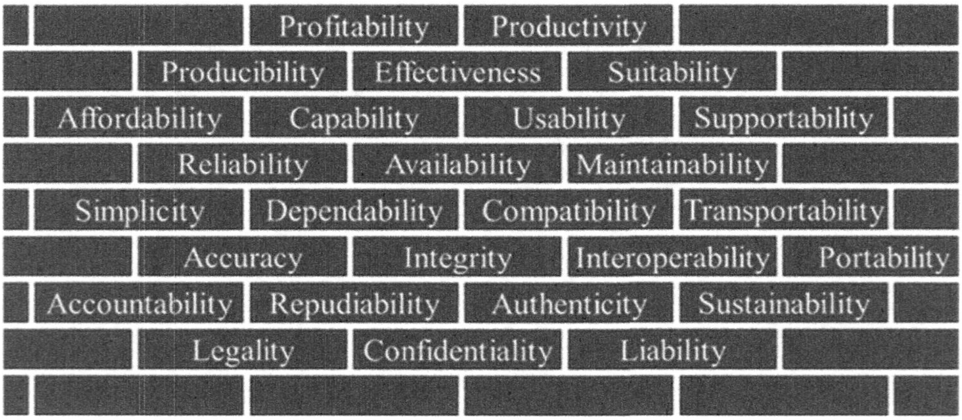

Figure 11-12. *Security Built as a Foundation Complete with the Systematic Development of Software*

Secure Development Life Cycle (SDL)

Secure coding has not been high on the list for most organizations. The rise in issues of malware and hackers has raised awareness of this issue significantly. First and foremost, recognition of the need to include secure coding principles into the development process is a common element despite the framework being used. For more information, read "What Is the Security Development Life Cycle"?[1]

The Software Assurance Forum for Excellence in Code (SAFECode) is an organization formed from some of the leading software development firms with the objective of advancing software assurance through better development methods. Visit SAFECode.[2] Regardless of the software development process used, the first step down the path to secure coding is to apply secure coding principles.

SDL accounts for security in each of its four major phases: requirements phase, design phase, coding phase, and testing phase.

Requirements Phase

This phase should define the specific security requirements if they are to be designed into the project. Secure coding does not refer to adding security functionality into a piece of software. The objective of the secure coding process is to properly implement all of the requirements so that the resultant software performs as advertised.

The requirements process is a key component of security in software development. Security-related items enumerated during the requirements process are visible throughout the rest of the software development process. They can be built into the systems and subsystems, addressed during coding, and tested. For the subsequent steps to be effective, the security requirements need to be both specific and positive.

During the requirements phase, there are numerous security issues that need to be considered. The cost of adding security later on in the development process rises exponentially as the process goes forward.

- Analysis of security and privacy risk

- Authentication and password management

- Audit logging and analysis

---

[1] www.microsoft.com/security/sdl/default.aspx
[2] www.safecode.org/

- Authorization and role management

- Data validation and sanitization

- Cryptography and key management

- Code integrity and validation testing

- Network and data security

- Ongoing education and awareness

- Team staffing requirements

- Third-party component analysis

Design Phase

Coding without designing first is like building a house without using plans. This might work fine on small projects, but as the scope grows, so do complexity and the opportunity for failure. Designing a software project is a multifaceted process.

There are two secure coding principles that can be applied at design time that can have a large influence on the code quality.

1. The first of these is the concept of *minimizing attack surface area.* Reducing the avenues of attack available to a hacker can have obvious benefits to the software. Minimizing attack surface area is a concept that tends to run counter to the way software has been designed—most designs come as a result of incremental accumulation, adding features and functions without regard to maintainability.

2. Threat modeling is a communication tool designed to communicate to everyone on the development team the threats and dangers facing the code. Define the scope by communicating what is in scope and out of scope with respect to the threat modeling effort. This includes both attacks and software components.

Enumerate assets by listing all of the component parts of the software being examined:

1. Decompose assets by breaking apart the software into small subsystems composed of inputs and outputs to simplify data flow analysis and to capture internal entry points.

2. Enumerate threats by listing all the threats to the software.

3. Classify the threats by their mode of operation.

4. Associate threats to assets by connecting specific threats and modes to specific software subsystems.

5. Score each specific threat–asset pair, and then rank them from most dangerous to least dangerous.

6. Create threat trees using a graphical representation of the required elements for an attack vector.

7. Score the mitigation efforts associated with each attack vector.

For more details on threat modeling, see "SDL Threat Modeling Tool."[3]

Coding Phase

The point at which the design is implemented is the coding phase in the software development process. There are two types of errors: the failure to include desired functionality and the inclusion of undesired behavior in the code. Testing for the first type of error is relatively easy if the requirements are enumerated in a previous phase of the process.

Testing for the inclusion of undesired behavior is significantly more difficult. Enumerations of known software weaknesses and vulnerabilities have been compiled and published as the Common Weakness Enumeration (CWE) and Common Vulnerabilities and Exposures (CVE) by the Mitre Corporation. The CVE and CWE are vendor- and language-neutral methods of describing errors. These enumerations allow a common vocabulary for communication about weaknesses and vulnerabilities. This common vocabulary has also led to the development of automated tools to manage the tracking of these issues.

Currently, the CWE describes more than 750 different weaknesses, far too many for developer memory and direct knowledge.

---

[3]www.microsoft.com/security/sdl/adopt/threatmodeling.aspx

Major Programming Errors

Mitre has collaborated with SANS to develop the CWE/SANS Top 25 Most Dangerous Programming Errors list. One of the ideas behind the Top 25 list is that it can be updated periodically as the threat landscape changes. Explore the current listing: "2019 CWE/SANS Top 25 Most Dangerous Software Errors."[4]

The current Top 25 list is divided into three high-level categories: Insecure Interactions Between Components, Risky Resource Management, and Porous Defenses. The Top 25 list covers a wide range of programs, from software application programs to web applications and across a wide range of programming skill levels.

Buffer Overflows

The CERT/CC at Carnegie Mellon University estimates that nearly half of all exploits of computer programs stem historically from some form of buffer overflow. The generic classification of buffer overflows includes many variants, such as static buffer overruns, indexing errors, format string bugs, Unicode and ANSI buffer size mismatches, and heap overruns.

The first line of defense is to write solid code. Regardless of the language used, or the source of outside input, prudent programming practice is to treat all input from outside a function as hostile. Validate all inputs as if they were hostile, and attempt to force a buffer overflow. With the amount of attention paid to this type of vulnerability, its presence is significantly reduced in newly discovered vulnerabilities.

Software Vulnerabilities

In today's computing environment, a wide range of character sets is used. Unicode allows multi-language support. Character code sets allow multi-language capability. Various encoding schemes, such as hex encoding, are supported to allow diverse inputs. The net result of all these input methods is that there are numerous ways to create the same input to a program.

---

[4]https://cwe.mitre.org/top25/archive/2019/2019_cwe_top25.html

Canonicalization is the process by which application programs manipulate strings to a base form, creating a foundational representation of the input. Canonicalization errors arise from the fact that inputs to a web application may be processed by multiple applications, such as web server, application server, and database server, each with its own parsers to resolve appropriate canonicalization issues.

Injections

The use of input to a function without validation has already been shown to be risky behavior. Another issue with un-validated input is the case of code injection. Rather than the input being appropriate for the function, this code injection changes the function in an unintended way. An SQL injection attack is a form of code injection aimed at any Structured Query Language (SQL)-based database.

Testing for SQL Injection Vulnerability

There are two main steps associated with testing for SQL injection vulnerability (Figure 11-13).

1.   You need to confirm that the system is at all vulnerable.

2.   Use the error message information to attempt to perform an actual exploit against the database.

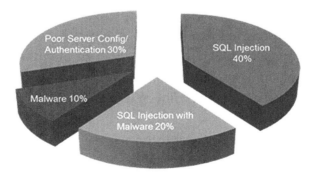

Figure 11-13. *SQL Injection Vulnerability*

Least Privilege

Whenever the software accesses a file, a system component, or another program, the issue of appropriate access control needs to be addressed. And although the simple practice of just giving everything root or administrative access may solve this immediate problem, it creates much bigger security issues that will be much less apparent in the future:

1.   The developer must understand what privileges are required specifically for an application to execute and access all its required resources.

2.   Determine what needs to be accessed and what the appropriate level of permission is; then use that level in design and implementation.

Testing Phase

The testing phase is the last opportunity to determine that the software performs properly before the end user experiences problems. Errors found in testing are late in the development process, but at least they are still learned about internally, before the product is released. Testing can occur at each level of development: module, subsystem, system, and completed application. The sooner errors are discovered and corrected, the lower the cost and the lesser the impact will be to project schedules. This makes testing an essential step in the process of developing good programs.

One of the most powerful tools that can be used in testing is fuzzing, the systematic application of a series of malformed inputs to test how the program responds. Fuzzing has been used by hackers for years to find potentially exploitable buffer overflows, without any specific knowledge of the coding. A tester can use a fuzzing framework to automate numerous input sequences.

Each one of the testing methodologies listed below is used for different objectives. The difference among white-, gray-, and black-box testing is the amount of access to the design and code elements. Penetration testing is designed to test configuration, security controls, and common defenses. Penetration testing can explore whether or not specific security controls can be bypassed.

White-box: Test team has access to the design and coding elements.

Grey-box: Test team has more information than in black-box testing but not as much as in white-box testing.

Black-box: Test team does not have access to design and coding elements.

Penetration: Designed to test configuration, security controls, and common defenses.

Summary

In this chapter you learned about the importance of securing a system. It is important to know what type of applications will be required and which products and/or services are needed. Becoming aware of what the functional specifications are for software to be satisfactory will help to be informed of the means needed to implement procedures needed to establish host security.

Resources

- **Security Development Life Cycle**: `www.microsoft.com/security/sdl/default.aspx`

- **SAFECode**: `www.safecode.org/`

CHAPTER 12

Email, Instant Messaging, and Web Components

You probably send and receive email every day. With the popularity of email, there also comes the issue of security concerns. Due to the everyday use of technologies such as email and instant messaging, many users may overlook or not be aware of the security issues associated with these technologies. In this chapter you will learn about security issues relating to email, instant messaging, and web-based applications.

By the end of this chapter, you will be able to

1. Describe security issues associated with email and instant messaging.

2. Explain web applications, plug-ins, and related security issues.

3. Explain web-based application security issues.

Security of Email

Server-based and desktop-based virus protection can help against malicious code (Figure 12-1). Spam filters attempt to block all unsolicited commercial email. Security of email depends on three protocols: Simple Mail Transfer Protocol (SMTP),[1] Post Office Protocol version 3 (POP3),[2] and Internet Message Access Protocol (IMAP).[3] Hypertext Transfer Protocol (HTTP) is also used for accessing email.

---

[1]www.geeksforgeeks.org/simple-mail-transfer-protocol-smtp/
[2]https://whatis.techtarget.com/definition/POP3-Post-Office-Protocol-3
[3]https://whatis.techtarget.com/definition/IMAP-Internet-Message-Access-Protocol

© Ahmed F. Sheikh 2020
A. F Sheikh, *CompTIA Security+ Certification Study Guide*, https://doi.org/10.1007/978-1-4842-6234-4_12

You can help protect your system from an infestation via email by scanning your email using your antivirus software, disabling your preview pane in your client email, following safe practices and procedures, and educating employees on best practices.

Figure 12-1. AVG Antivirus Free Edition Software: Screenshot of Running a Scan

Hoax Emails

Forwarding hoax emails and other jokes, funny movies, and nonwork-related emails at work can be a violation of your company's acceptable use policy and result in disciplinary actions. Visit Snopes,[4] a site that debunks hoaxes, for information.

---

[4]www.snopes.com/

Spam

The junk mail of email is referred to as spam or unsolicited commercial email. Almost all email providers filter spam. Unfortunately, spam still consumes bandwidth as it is being sent and the recipient's server still has to process the message. Methods for dealing with spam include email filtering, educating the user about being cautious toward unknown email(s), shutting down open relays, greylisting,[5] blacklisting or DNSBL,[6] and using host/server filters.

Mail Encryption

Email is sent in clear text unless the message or the attachments have been purposefully encrypted. To provide confidentiality, email content encryption methods include Secure/Multipurpose Internet Mail Extensions (S/MIME) and Pretty Good Privacy (PGP).

S/MIME

S/MIME was created to allow Internet email to support new and more creative features. The original email RFC specified only text email, so any non-text data had to be handled by a new specification. MIME[7] allows email to handle multiple types of content in a message and handles audio files, images, applications, and multipart emails.

S/MIME was developed by RSA Data Security and uses the X.509 format for certificates. The specification supports both 40-bit RC2 and 3DES for symmetric encryption. The protocol can affect the message in one of two ways: the host mail program can encode the message with S/MIME, or the server can act as the processing agent, encrypting all messages between servers.

---

[5]https://support.threattracksecurity.com/support/solutions/articles/1000070643-what-is-greylisting-and-how-does-it-work-
[6]www.dnsbl.info/#:~:text=What%20is%20a%20DNSBL%3F,a%20history%20of%20sending%20spam.
[7]https://whatis.techtarget.com/definition/MIME-Multi-Purpose-Internet-Mail-Extensions

Configuration Settings in Outlook

Several popular email programs support S/MIME. They manage S/MIME keys and functions through the Email Security screen as shown in Figure 12-2. There are different settings that can be used to encrypt messages and use X.509 digital certificates. This allows interoperability with web certificates, and trusted authorities are available to issue the certificates. Trusted authorities are needed to ensure the senders are who they claim to be, an important part of authentication.

While S/MIME is a good and versatile protocol for securing email, its implementation can be problematic. S/MIME allows the user to select low-strength (40 bit) encryption, which means a user can send a message that is thought to be secure but that can be more easily decoded than messages sent with 3DES encryption. Also, as with any protocol, bugs can exist in the software itself. See Figure 12-3.

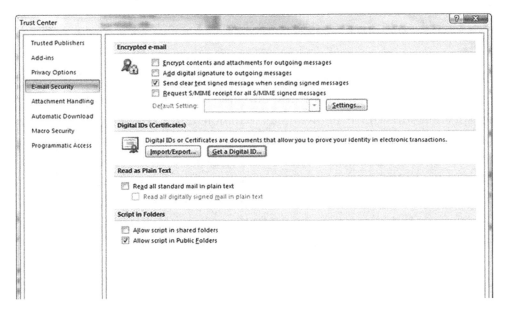

Figure 12-2. *Screenshot of S/MIME Options in Outlook*

Figure 12-3. *Screenshot of S/MIME Options in Windows Mail*

Pretty Good Privacy (PGP)

PGP implements email security in a similar fashion to S/MIME but uses completely different protocols.

PGP framework

- Using PGP, the user sends the email, and the mail agent applies encryption as specified per the programming.

- The content is encrypted with the symmetric key, and that key is encrypted with the public key of the recipient of the email for confidentiality.

- PGP manages keys locally in its own software. A free key server is available for storing PGP public keys.

Instant Messaging

The protocols used for these chat applications have default TCP ports—AIM uses 5190, Jabber uses 5222 and 5269, Yahoo Messenger uses 5050, and MSN/Windows Live Messenger uses 1863. For an instant message system to work properly, you will want to

1. Announce your presence on the server.

2. Attach to a server (typically announcing the IP address of the originating client).

Please see Figure 12-4 for an illustration.

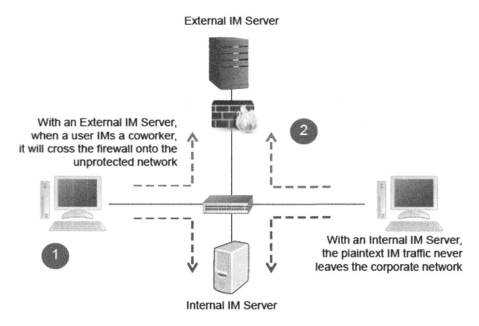

Figure 12-4. *Instant Messaging*

Web Components

As you continue this chapter, you will learn about components used on the Web to request and deliver information securely over the Internet. The usefulness of the Web is not due just to browsers but also to web components that enable services for end users through their browser interfaces. These components use a wide range of protocols and services to deliver the desired content to end users. They are easy to use and offer a secure method of conducting data transfers over the Internet. Many protocols have been developed to deliver this content, although for most users, the browser handles the details.

Current Web Components and Concerns

From a systems point of view, many security concerns have arisen, but they can be grouped into three main tasks:

- Securing a server that delivers content to users over the Web

- Securing the transport of information between users

- Servers over the Web securing the user's computer from attack over a web connection

Take a closer look at the various protocols, shown in Figure 12-5, used on the Web:

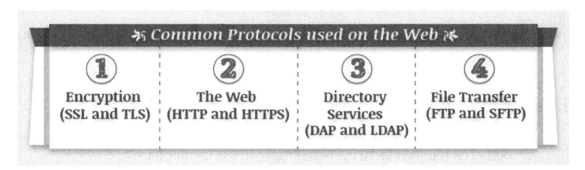

Figure 12-5. *Common Protocols Used on the Web*

1. **Encryption (SSL and TLS)**: Secure Socket Layer (SSL) manages encryption, thus providing confidentiality, while Transport Layer Security (TLS) prevents eavesdropping and tampering. Both protocols are configured in the browser. See Figure 12-6.

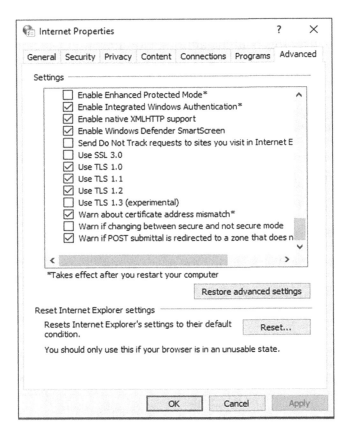

Figure 12-6. *Internet Options Display Where Both SSL and TLS Protocols Are Configured*

SSL/TLS Handshake: At the beginning of an SSL session, an SSL handshake is performed which sets up the cryptographic parameters of the session. For details of the steps of an SSL handshake and an illustration, see "An Overview of the SSL Handshake."[8]

How SSL/TLS Works: Authentication was a one-way process for SSL v1 and SSL v2, with only the server providing authentication. In SSL v3/TLS, mutual authentication of both client and server is possible.

---

[8]www.ibm.com/support/knowledgecenter/SSFKSJ/com.ibm.mq.helphome.doc/product_welcome_wmq.htm

The process always begins with a client request for a secure connection and a server's response. For the client and server to communicate, both sides must agree on a commonly held protocol (SSL v1, SSL v2, SSL v3, or TLS v1). Commonly available cryptographic algorithms include Diffie–Hellman and RSA.

The next step is to exchange certificates and keys as necessary to enable authentication. The channel is protected by encryption against eavesdropping. Each packet is encrypted using the symmetric key before transfer across the network and then decrypted by the receiver.

SSL/TLS Attacks: SSL/TLS is specifically designed to provide protection from man-in-the middle attacks, but a Trojan program that copies keystrokes and echoes them to another TCP/IP address in parallel with the intended communication can defeat SSL/TLS. The Trojan program must copy the data prior to SSL/TLS encapsulation. This type of attack has occurred and has been used to steal passwords and other sensitive material from users, performing the theft as the user actually types in the data.

2. **The Web (HTTP and HTTPS)**: HTTPS (HTTP over SSL) uses TCP Port 443. The unencrypted form is Hypertext Transfer Protocol (HTTP), which uses TCP Port 80.

   You should always verify that a secure connection has been established when entering sensitive information at a website. In the example in Figure 12-7, notice that the link in the browser begins with https which indicates that a secure connection has been established.

Figure 12-7. *Example Includes a Web Link That Begins with HTTPS*

3. **Directory Services (DAP and LDAP)**: A directory is a data storage mechanism designed to provide efficient data retrieval services. The data is hierarchically described in a treelike structure, and a network interface for reading is typical. See Figure 12-8. To enable interoperability, the X.500 standard was created as a standard for directory services. Lightweight Directory Access Protocol, or LDAP, can interface with X.500 services. Client programs that are LDAP-aware like an email client can ask LDAP servers to look up entries. LDAP servers index all of the data in their entries and use filters to select the requested data. LDAP is used to look up encryption certificates or pointers to printers.

SSL/TLS provides several important functions to LDAP:

- Establishes the identity of a data source through the use of certificates

- Provides for the integrity and confidentiality of the data being presented from an LDAP source

To achieve LDAP over SSL/TLS, the typical setup is to establish an SSL/TLS connection, and then open an LDAP connection over the protected channel. A directory is designed and optimized for reading data, offering very fast search and retrieval operations. LDAP offers all of the functionality most directories need and is easier and more economical to implement.

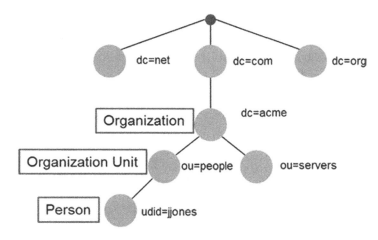

Figure 12-8. *Directory Services*

4. **File Transfer (FTP and SFTP):** File Transfer Protocol (FTP) is a
    standard network protocol used to exchange and manipulate files
    over a TCP/IP-based network. FTP transfers files in plain text and
    is an application-level protocol that operates over a wide range of
    lower-level protocols. FTP is embedded in most operating systems
    and provides a method of transferring files from a sender to a
    receiver and can be used from a command line interface. Secure
    FTP (SFTP) is used when confidential transfer is required and
    combines both the Secure Shell (SSH) protocol and FTP. FTP over
    SSL (FTPS) uses TCP Port 990 and TCP Port 989. The unencrypted
    form is File Transfer Protocol (FTP), which uses TCP Port 21 and
    TCP Port 20.

Buffer Overflows

Since a lot of forms are used at websites, buffer overflows can pose a security concern.
You will recall that a buffer overflow is the result of poor coding practices by the software
programmer. An application accepts more input than it has assigned storage space, and
the input data overwrites other program areas. See Figure 12-9.

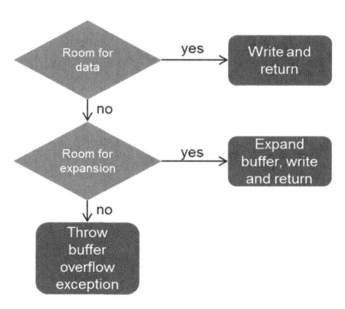

Figure 12-9. *Illustration of Process Occurring in Buffer Overflow*

Java

Java is a platform-independent, object-oriented programming language. Java uses a Java virtual machine to run the application and is one of the most popular programming languages. Java adds an interactive element to websites. See Figure 12-10.

Figure 12-10. *Security Settings— Internet Zone*

JavaScript

JavaScript is a scripting language rather than a programming language and was developed to be operated within a browser instance. Java enables features such as validation of forms. JavaScript is also used to add interactivity to web pages. The script can either be embedded in the web page or downloaded from the web server. The browser interprets and runs the JavaScript.

ActiveX

ActiveX technology can be used to create complex application logic that is then embedded into other container objects such as a web browser. ActiveX components have very significant capabilities, and thus malicious ActiveX objects can be very dangerous. The ActiveX software framework was developed by Microsoft. See Figure 12-11.

ActiveX can

- Be used to download and execute code automatically over an Internet-based channel.

- Enable a browser to display a custom type of information in a particular way.

- Perform tasks such as update the operating system and application programs.

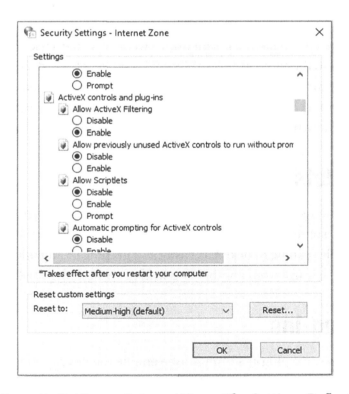

Figure 12-11. *Security Settings—Internet Zone. The Settings Reflect the ActiveX Controls and Plug-ins*

CGI and Server-Side Scripts

The **Common Gateway Interface (CGI)** was the original method that a web server used to execute a program. The intent was to pass information via environment variables to an independent program, execute the program, and return the results to the web server for display. Sometimes scripts appear to be fine, but unexpected user inputs can have unintended consequences.

CGI has been replaced in many websites through newer **server-side scripting** technologies such as Java, **Active Server Pages (ASP)**, **ASP.NET**, and **PHP**. All these technologies operate in much the same way as CGI. They all allow programs to be run outside the web server and to return data to the web server to be served to end users via a web page. Each of these newer technologies has advantages and disadvantages, but all of them have stronger security models than CGI.

Cookies

A cookie is a small piece of data that is sent from a website, while a user browses a website. If the user goes back to the same website, the cookie can be retrieved. For example, if you log-in to a website, your credentials are carried throughout the site as you click from page to page. Cookies cannot carry viruses or install malware, but tracking cookies can create a record or an individual's browsing habits.

Signed Applets

A signed applet contains a signature that the browser verifies through an independent certificate authority server. Once a signature is verified, a signed applet can get increased rights. A signed applet can be hijacked as easily as a graphic or any other file. Inline is using an embedded control from another site with or without the other site's permission.

Browser Plug-ins

The Flash and Shockwave plug-ins from Adobe enable the development of interesting graphic and cartoon animations that greatly enhance the look and feel of a web page. The plug-in is required to display the content developed using the appropriate software. Dynamic data such as movies and music can be manipulated by a wide variety of plug-ins.

Until recently, plug-ins had a remarkable safety record. As Flash-based content has grown more popular, crackers have examined the Flash plug-ins and software, determined vulnerabilities, and developed exploit code to use against the Flash protocol. Adobe has patched the issue, but as more and more third-party plug-ins become popular, expect data losses to occur as crackers investigate the more popular plug-ins and protocols for vulnerabilities.

Open Vulnerability and Assessment Language (OVAL)

The Mitre Corporation, a government-funded research group, has compiled a library of vulnerabilities, the Common Vulnerabilities and Exposures (CVE), which is a system that provides a reference method for publicly known information security vulnerabilities and exposures. The CVE led to efforts such as the development of the Open Vulnerability and Assessment Language (OVAL).[9] OVAL comprises two main elements: an XML-based machine-readable language for describing vulnerabilities and a repository.

Web 2.0 and Security

A Web 2.0 site allows users to interact and collaborate with each other. Social networking sites, blogs, wikis, and video sharing sites are all examples of Web 2.0. Internet privacy is a growing concern with the growth of Web 2.0 technologies.

Summary

In this chapter you learned about security issues relating to both email and instant messaging. You had the opportunity to review the process of encrypting emails and configuring settings to establish safeguards against potential security threats. In this chapter you had the opportunity to learn about common protocols used on the Web which support security and the Open Vulnerability and Assessment Language which serves as a reference method for publicly known information security vulnerabilities.

---

[9]http://oval.mitre.org/

Resources

- **Simple Mail Transfer Protocol**: www.geeksforgeeks.org/simple-mail-transfer-protocol-smtp/

- **Post Office Protocol version 3**: https://whatis.techtarget.com/definition/POP3-Post-Office-Protocol-3

- **Internet Message Access Protocol**: https://whatis.techtarget.com/definition/IMAP-Internet-Message-Access-Protocol

- **Snopes**: www.snopes.com/

- **Greylisting**: https://support.threattracksecurity.com/support/solutions/articles/1000070643-what-is-greylisting-and-how-does-it-work-

- **Blacklisting or DNSBL**: www.dnsbl.info/#:~:text=What%20is%20a%20DNSBL%3F,a%20history%20of%20sending%20spam.

- **MIME**: https://whatis.techtarget.com/definition/MIME-Multi-Purpose-Internet-Mail-Extensions

- **Open Vulnerability and Assessment Language**: http://oval.mitre.org/

CHAPTER 13

Authentication and Remote Access

In this chapter you will gain an understanding of authentication and remote access. You will learn about the function and purpose of authentication service, about the best practices relating to authentication, and about the methods and protocols used for remote access to networks.

By the end of this chapter, you will be able to

1. Explain the function and purpose of authentication services.

2. Explain the fundamental concepts and best practices related to authentication.

3. Identify the methods and protocols used for remote access to networks.

Authentication and Remote Access

In this chapter, you will have the opportunity to learn about the various methods and protocols that can be used for remote access to networks. To establish proper privileges, three steps are used as shown in Figure 13-1.

© Ahmed F. Sheikh 2020
A. F Sheikh, *CompTIA Security+ Certification Study Guide*, https://doi.org/10.1007/978-1-4842-6234-4_13

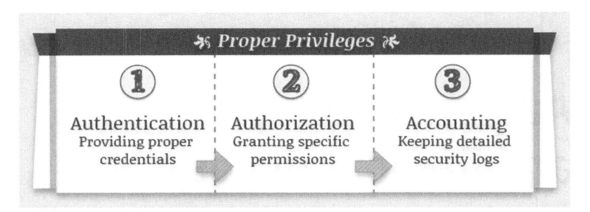

Figure 13-1. *Proper Privileges*

1. **Authentication**: Authentication is the matching of user-supplied credentials to previously stored credentials on a host machine, and it usually involves an account username and password.

2. **Authorization**: After the proper credentials are provided and the user is authenticated, authorization grants specific permissions based on the privileges held by the user account. Permission to use the network, print to a printer, or to use specific applications such as FTP are examples of permissions which can be set. Authorization is a function of the operating system in conjunction with its established security policies.

3. **Accounting**: Accounting is the collection of billing and other detailed records. Network access is often a billable function, and a log of how much time, bandwidth, file transfer space, or other resources were used can be maintained. Other accounting functions include keeping detailed security logs to maintain an audit trail of tasks being performed.

Kerberos Operations

The name Kerberos comes from the multiheaded dog which guards the gates of the underworld in Greek mythology. Kerberos, the authentication protocol, uses strong encryption so that a client can prove its identity to a server and the server can in turn authenticate itself to the client.

The Kerberos server contains user IDs and hashed passwords for all users that will have authorizations to realm services. The Kerberos server also has shared secret keys with every server to which it will grant access tickets. The basis for authentication in a Kerberos environment is the ticket. Tickets are used in a two-step process with the client. The first ticket is a *ticket-granting ticket* (TGT) issued by the authentication service (AS) to a requesting client. The client can then present this ticket to the Kerberos server with a request for a ticket to access a specific server.

This *client-to-server ticket* (also called a *service ticket*) is used to gain access to a server's service. Since the entire session can be encrypted, this eliminates the inherently insecure transmission of items such as a password that can be intercepted on the network. Tickets are time-stamped and have a lifetime, so attempting to reuse a ticket will not be successful.

To illustrate how the Kerberos authentication service works, think about your driver's license. See Figure 13-2. You can present your license to other parties to prove you are who you claim to be. Because other parties trust the state in which the license was issued, they will accept your license as proof of your identity.

The state in which the license was issued is analogous to the Kerberos authentication service, and the license acts as a client-to-server ticket.

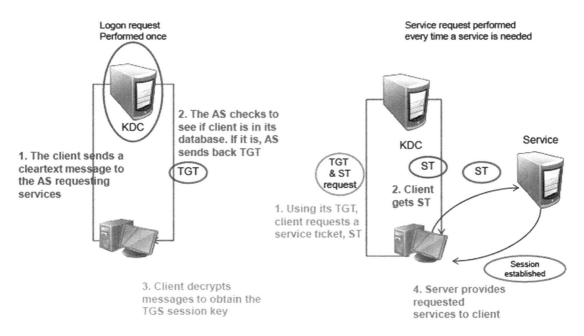

***Figure 13-2.** Kerberos Operation*

Mutual Authentication

Mutual authentication is a two-way authentication used so that both parties are assured of the other's identity. A user authenticates to a server and that server also authenticates itself to the user. See Figure 13-3 for an example of the process that occurs between the client and the server. Once verification is established between the client and server, data is transferred.

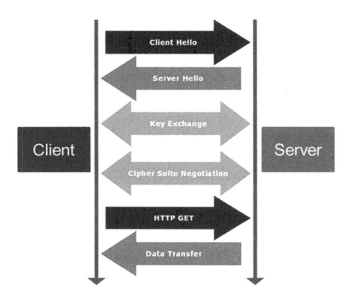

Figure 13-3. *Mutual Authentication*

Domains

A security domain is the resources within a domain that are operating under the same security policy. This set of resources is available to a subject. There are several frameworks available that describe access control rules which use security labels on objects and clearances for subjects. For example, I may not have the required clearance to access a document that has been labeled as top secret.

Models of Access Control/Discretionary Access Control

Both discretionary access control and mandatory access control are terms originally used by the military to describe two different approaches to controlling what access an individual has on a system. See Figure 13-4.

In systems that employ discretionary access controls, the owner of an object can decide which other subjects may have access to the object and what specific access they may have. One common method to accomplish this is with permissions. The owner of a file can specify what permissions (read/write/execute) members in the same group may have and also what permissions all others may have. Access control lists are another common mechanism used to implement discretionary access control.

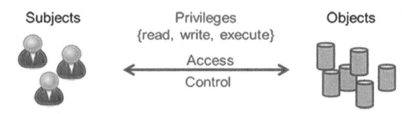

Figure 13-4. *Illustration of Models of Access and Discretionary Access Control*

Models of Access Control Mandatory Access Control

A less frequently employed system for restricting access is mandatory access control. This system, generally used only in environments where different levels of security classifications exist, is much more restrictive of what a user is allowed to do. It is important to have a foundational understanding of the term mandatory access control review definition here.[1]

In the case of MAC, the owner or subject cannot determine whether access is to be granted to another subject; it is the job of the operating system to decide. The security mechanism controls access to all objects, and individual subjects cannot change that access. The key here is the label attached to every subject and object. The label identifies the level of classification for that object and the level that the subject is entitled to.

---

[1]https://searchsecurity.techtarget.com/definition/mandatory-access-control-MAC

Think of military security classifications such as Secret and Top Secret. A file that has been identified as Top Secret (has a label indicating that it is Top Secret) may be viewed only by individuals with a Top Secret clearance. It is up to the access control mechanism to ensure that an individual with only a Secret clearance never gains access to a file labeled as Top Secret. Similarly, a user cleared for Top Secret access will not be allowed by the access control mechanism to change the classification of a file labeled as Top Secret to Secret or to send that Top Secret file to a user cleared only for Secret information.

Models of Access Control: Role-Based Access Control

Another access control mechanism is role-based access control or RBAC. In this scheme, the user is assigned a set of roles that the user may perform. The roles are in turn assigned the access permissions necessary to perform the tasks associated with the role. Users will thus be granted permissions to objects in terms of the specific duties they must perform—not of a security classification associated with individual objects.

Models of Access Control: Rule-Based Access Control

Rule-based access control also uses objects such as access control lists (ACLs) to help determine whether or not access should be granted, but in this case, a series of rules is contained in the ACL, and the determination of whether to grant access is made based on these rules. An example of such a rule is one that states that no employee may have access to the payroll file after hours or on weekends.

As with MAC, users are not allowed to change the access rules, and administrators are relied on to enforce this. Rule-based access control can actually be used in addition to or as a method of implementing other access control methods. For example, MAC methods can utilize a rule-based approach for implementation.

Remote Access Protocols

IEEE 802.1x

This standard describes methods used to authenticate a user prior to granting access to the network and the authentication server, such as a RADIUS server. 802.1X acts through an intermediate device, such as an edge switch, enabling ports to carry normal traffic if the connection is properly authenticated. This prevents unauthorized clients from accessing the publicly available ports on a switch, keeping unauthorized users out of a LAN.

EAP is a general protocol that can support multiple methods of authentication, including one-time passwords, Kerberos, public keys, and security device methods such as smart cards.

Once a client successfully authenticates itself to the 802.1X device, the switch opens ports for normal traffic. At this point, the client can communicate with the system's AAA method, such as a RADIUS server, and authenticate itself to the network. The illustration (Figure 13-5) provided reflects the remote access protocol process described earlier.

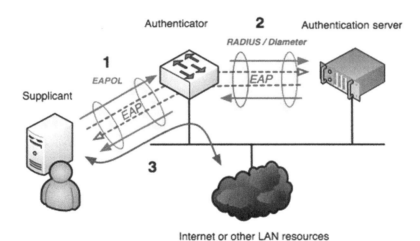

Figure 13-5. *Remote Access Protocol Using IEEE 802.1x*

RADIUS

Remote Authentication Dial-In User Service, or RADIUS, is a client/server protocol that uses port 1813 to provide centralized authentication, authorization, and accounting for computers to connect and use the available network services.

Review the following characteristics specific to RADIUS:

- Authentication, Authorization, and Accounting (AAA) Protocol

- Connectionless

- Uses the User Datagram Protocol (UDP) as its transport layer protocol

- A client/server protocol

In order to best illustrate the process that occurs during a remote access using RADIUS, an outline presented here details the process, and Figure 13-6 illustrates the steps provided:

1. User initiates Point-to-Point Protocol (PPP) connection to Network-Attached Storage (NAS).

2. NAS prompts user for credentials.

3. User replies to NAS with credentials.

4. RADIUS client sends username and encrypted password to RADIUS server.

5. RADIUS responds

   - Access–Accept

   - Access–Reject

   - Access–Challenge

6. RADIUS client acts upon AAA rules allowing access to remote resources.

The RADIUS protocol has evolved into the Diameter protocol which is an application layer protocol and provides AAA services.

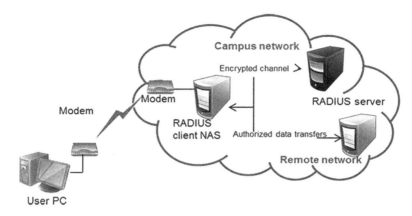

Figure 13-6. *Remote Access Protocol Using RADIUS*

TACACS+

The Terminal Access Controller Access Control System+ (TACACS+) has extended attribute control and accounting processes. One of the fundamental design aspects is the separation of authentication, authorization, and accounting in this protocol.

TACACS+ uses TCP as its transport protocol, typically operating over TCP port 49. This port is used for the log-in process. TACACS+ can also use UDP as its transport protocol. Communications between a TACACS+ client and TACACS+ server are encrypted using a shared secret that is manually configured into each entity and is not shared over a connection.

Hence, communications between a TACACS+ client (typically a NAS) and a TACACS+ server are secure, but the communications between a user (typically a PC) and the TACACS+ client are subject to compromise.

Please review the detailed steps provided which outline the remote access process using TACACS+ and the illustration (Figure 13-7) which depicts the following steps:

1. User initiates PPP connection to NAS.

2. NAS prompts user for credentials.

3. User replies to NAS with credentials.

4. TACACS+ client START request.

5. TACACS+ server replies:

    • Complete authentication

    • Client sending CONTINUE and loop until complete

6. TACACS+ client and server authorization requests.

7. TACACS+ client acts upon AAA rules to permit access to remote
    resources.

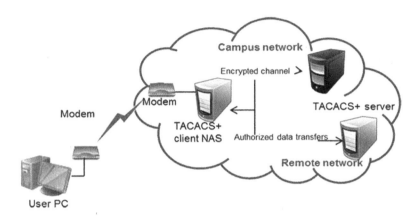

Figure 13-7. *Remote Access Protocol Using TACAS+*

Secure Shell (SSH)

SSH is a protocol series designed to facilitate secure network functions across an
insecure network. See Figure 13-8. SSH is the secure alternative for the insecure Telnet
application. Telnet allowed users to connect between systems. Although Telnet is still
used, it has some drawbacks.

SSH opens a secure transport channel between machines by using an SSH daemon
on each end. These daemons initiate contact over TCP port 22 and then communicate
over higher ports in a secure mode. One of the strengths of SSH is its support for many
different encryption protocols.

The SSH protocol has facilities to encrypt data automatically, provide authentication,
and compress data in transit. The protocol is designed to be flexible and simple, and it is
designed specifically to minimize the number of round trips between systems. The key
exchange, public key, symmetric key, message authentication, and hash algorithms are
all negotiated at connection time. Individual data packet integrity is assured through

the use of a message authentication code that is computed from a shared secret, the contents of the packet, and the packet sequence number.

There are three major components

- Transport layer protocol

- User authentication protocol

- Connection protocol

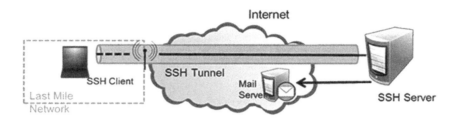

Figure 13-8. *Remote Access Protocol Using SSH*

Virtual Private Network

A virtual private network (VPN) is a secure virtual network that uses the public network (i.e., the Internet). The security of a VPN lies in the encryption of packet content between the endpoints that define the VPN.

Because the packet contents between VPN endpoints are encrypted, to an outside observer on the public network, the communication is secure, and depending on how the VPN is set up, security can even extend to the two communicating parties' machines.

An example of VPN setup could be comprised of multiple regional offices, remote roaming users, and the head office. Figure 13-9 illustrates this VPN scenario.

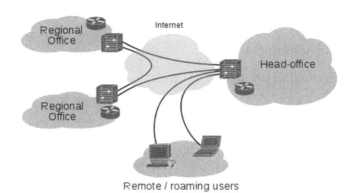

Figure 13-9. *Virtual Private Network*

Internet Protocol Security (IPsec)

IPsec operates at the Open Systems Interconnection (OSI) model Layer 3, the network layer, and provides content and context protection. IPsec provides a sweeping array of services:

- Access control
- Connectionless integrity
- Traffic flow confidentiality
- Rejection of replayed packets
- Data security (encryption)

IPsec can be executed in a transport or tunnel mode:

Transport Mode: In transport mode, end-to-end security of packet traffic is provided by the endpoint computers.

The transport method encrypts only the data portion of a packet, thus enabling an outsider to see source and destination IP addresses. The transport method protects the higher-level protocols associated with a packet and protects the data being transmitted but allows knowledge of the transmission itself.

Tunneling Mode: In tunnel mode (portal-to-portal), security of packet traffic is provided between endpoint node machines in each network and not at the terminal host machines.

Tunneling provides encryption of source and destination IP addresses, as well as of the data itself. This provides the greatest security, but it can be done only between IPSec servers (or routers) because the final destination needs to be known for delivery.

It is possible to use both the transport and tunnel methods at the same time. You can use transport within your own network to reach an IPSec server, which then tunnels to the target server's network, connecting to an IPSec server there, and then using the transport method from the target network's IPSec server to the target host.

Four basic configurations can be applied to machine-to-machine connections using IPsec.

1. Host-to-host connection, wherein the Internet is not part of the SA between the machine.

2. Two security devices in the stream secure the network between them.

3. A combination of the first two configurations.

4. User establishes an SA with the security gateway and then a separate SA with the desired server

Summary

In this chapter you learned about the fundamental concepts of authentication. You reviewed the authentication process, models of access control including role-based access control, and rule-based access control. You learned about the importance of implementing the appropriate type of methods and protocols needed for remote access to networks.

Resource

- **Mandatory Access Control**: https://searchsecurity.techtarget.com/definition/mandatory-access-control-MAC

CHAPTER 14

Access Control and Privilege Management

In this chapter you will learn about fundamental concepts along with best practices of authorization and access control. You will also gain an understanding of how to apply the correct security controls when managing accounts.

By the end of this chapter, you will be able to

1. Explain the fundamental concepts and best practices related to authorization and access control.

2. Implement appropriate security controls when performing account management.

Privilege Management

Privilege management is the process of setting restrictions on a user's ability to use network resources or control configuration parameters. Privilege management is handled by the operating system. In this chapter you will take a look at how this is accomplished by the various operating systems.

Windows 2019 Server Users

Since the Windows 2019 Server operating system centralizes user account management, users can be assigned to a group. Managing group permissions is much more efficient than trying to manage each user account individually. The Computer Management utility within the Windows operating system can be used to manage users and groups.

215

© Ahmed F. Sheikh 2020
A. F Sheikh, *CompTIA Security+ Certification Study Guide*, https://doi.org/10.1007/978-1-4842-6234-4_14

Group Management

Once a group is assigned permissions to access a particular resource, adding a new user to that group will allow the user to "inherit" the permissions of the group and grant the user permission to access that resource. See Figure 14-1.

Some operating systems, such as Windows, have built-in groups—groups that are already defined within the operating system, such as Administrators, Power Users, and Everyone. The whole concept of groups revolves around making the tasks of assigning and managing permissions easier, and built-in groups certainly help to make these tasks easier.

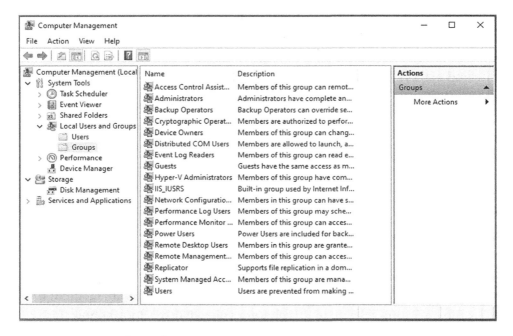

Figure 14-1. *Screenshot of a Computer Management Screen*

Password Policy Components

A *password policy* is a set of rules designed to enhance computer security by requiring users to employ and maintain strong passwords. A *domain password policy* is a password policy that applies to a specific domain.

1. **Password Construction**: A password policy requires users to employ and maintain strong passwords. Several components can be incorporated into the policy to enhance computer security. The number of characters a password should have and whether the use of capitalization, numbers, and special characters guide the user in constructing a password. Common words and personal information should be avoided.

2. **Reuse Restrictions and Duration**: Some organizations require that a password be changed every set number of days and that old passwords cannot be reused for a set period of time.

3. **Protection of Passwords**: Users are responsible for protecting their passwords. This includes not writing down passwords where others can find them, not saving passwords and not allowing automated logins, and not sharing passwords with other users, for example.

4. **Consequences**: The consequences of noncompliance should be spelled out as part of the policy.

For more information on password policies, go to SANS,[1] and type password policy into the search box.

Domain Password Policy Elements

Domains are logical groups of computers that share a central directory database. The Active Directory database is an example of a domain for recent Windows operating systems. The database contains information about the user accounts and security information for all resources identified within the domain.

A domain password policy is a password policy for a specific domain. Since these policies are usually associated with the Windows operating system, a domain password policy is implemented and enforced on the domain controller, which is a computer that responds to security authentication requests, such as logging in to a computer for a windows domain.

---

[1]www.sans.org/

The domain password policy usually falls under a group policy object and has the following elements: a password history, a maximum password age, a minimum password age, and complexity requirements, just as with the desktop version of the Windows operating system. However, with the NOS, you can store passwords using reversible encryption. This is a form of encryption that can easily be decrypted and is essentially the same as storing a plaintext version of the password (because it's so easy to reverse the encryption and get the password). This should be used only when applications use protocols that require the user's password for authentication (such as Challenge-Handshake Authentication Protocol or CHAP). See Figure 14-2.

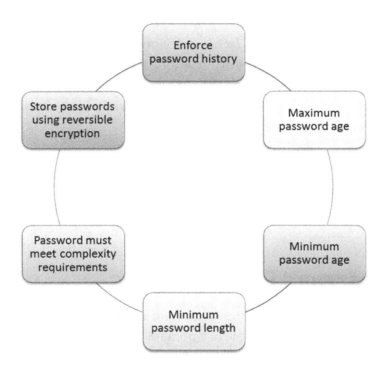

Figure 14-2. *Domain Password Policy Elements*

Single Sign-On (SSO)

Invariably, users will forget the passwords they chose for infrequently accessed systems, thus creating more work for system administrators who must assist users with password changes or password recovery efforts. To make remembering passwords easier, administrators utilize a technology called single sign-on.

Single sign-on allows a user to supply the right username and password once and have access to all the applications and data needed, without having to log in multiple times and remember many different passwords. From a user standpoint, SSO means you need to remember only one username and one password. From a security standpoint, single sign-on users are more likely to choose a complex password since they will only have to remember a single password.

The user signs in once, providing a username and password to the SSO server. The SSO server then provides authentication information to any resource the user accesses during that session. The server interfaces with the other applications and systems—the user does not need to log into each system individually. See Figure 14-3.

A downside here, though, is that if your credentials are compromised, all of the resources that use those credentials are at risk.

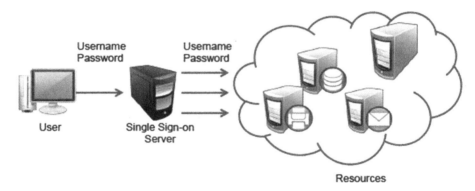

Figure 14-3. *Illustration of a Single Sign-On Process*

Time-of-Day Restrictions

Users can be restricted from logging in to the network at certain times. With these restrictions in place, you can enforce control of critical or sensitive resources. See Figure 14-4.

Figure 14-4. *Screenshot of the User Properties: Child Screen with Time Restrictions*

Setting Log-On Hours

In this example, users have been given round-the-clock, 24/7 access. This may be inappropriate for certain situations. An administrator may implement time-of-day restrictions on the accounts of clerks so that they may be logged in only from 8 AM to 6 PM. Monday through Saturday. See Figure 14-5 for an example of log-on hours permitted.

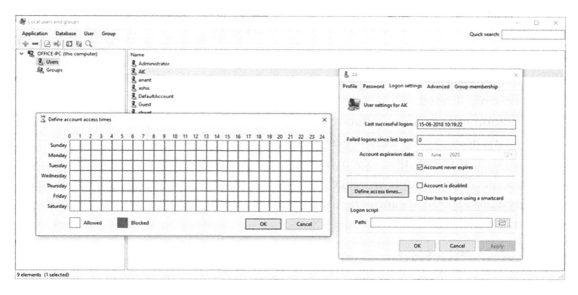

Figure 14-5. *Screenshot of Screen, Log-On Hours for Guest*

If a clerk attempts to log in outside the allowed hours, he/ she is denied access even if he/she supplies the proper authentication credentials. If a clerk is logged in when his/her allowable log-in time expires, the system can be configured to forcibly disconnect the clerk or just warn the clerk that his/her login hours have passed but still allow them to remain logged in.

Some operating systems give you the option of disconnecting users as soon as their "allowed log-on time" expires regardless of what the user is doing at the time. The more commonly used approach is to allow currently logged-in users to stay connected but reject any log-in attempts that occur outside of allowed hours.

Tokens

Usernames and passwords are something you know. Anyone who knows that same information can use those credentials. A more secure method of authentication is to combine the something you know with something you have. In some systems the token is a constantly changing number sequence which is synchronized to a remote server. When the user enters the correct username, password, and matching sequence of numbers, he is allowed to log in.

Account and Password Expiration

One of the best practices an organization can implement is to attach an expiration date to user passwords so that if an account is compromised, the time that it remains compromised is limited.

In addition to password expiration, password history mechanisms should be used. The history is used to keep track of previously used passwords so that they cannot be reused. Both are quite similar, except that password expiration is generally put in place because a specific account is intended for a specific purpose of limited duration. When an account has expired, it cannot be used unless the expiration deadline is extended.

Security Controls and Permissions

Permissions can be applied to specific users or groups to control that user's or group's ability to view, modify, access, use, or delete resources such as folders and files.

When using the New Technology File System (NTFS) in Windows, administrators can grant users and groups permission to perform certain tasks as they relate to files, folders, and registry keys.

- **Permissions** control what a user is allowed to do with objects on a system.

- **Rights** define the actions a user can perform on the system itself.

For an example of permissions for DATA, see Figure 14-6.

Figure 14-6. *Screenshot of Permissions for DATA Indicating the Group or User Names and the Permissions Allowed*

User Rights Assignment Options from Windows Local Security Settings

You can use the Local Security Policy utility to change user rights assignment options. User Rights Assignment policies determine which users or groups have log-on rights or privileges on the computer. See Figure 14-7.

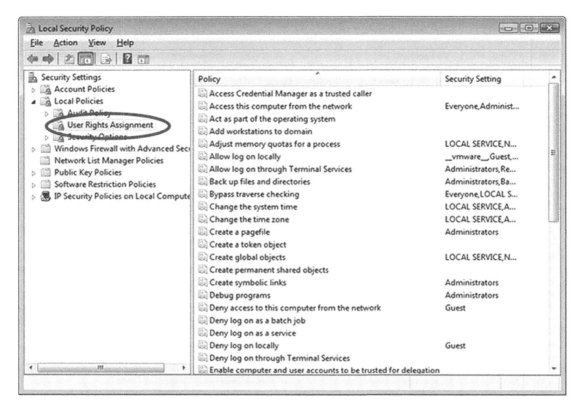

Figure 14-7. *Screenshot of a Local Security Policy with the User Rights Assignment Folder Highlighted*

Access Control Lists

Access control lists can be used to assign permissions for users and groups to access resources such as files and folders. See Figure 14-8. If a user is given only permission to read a file, they will not be able to make any changes to that file, but they can print the file out.

Figure 14-8. *Screenshot of Permissions for DATA Showing the Group or User Names and the Permissions Assigned*

Access Control

Access control is, as its name suggests, a way of controlling access to a building, to a room, to a system, or to a file. As you continue on with this chapter, you will take a look at the various methods that can be implemented to control access.

Access control can be broken down into different layers (Figure 14-9) that can actually work in concert.

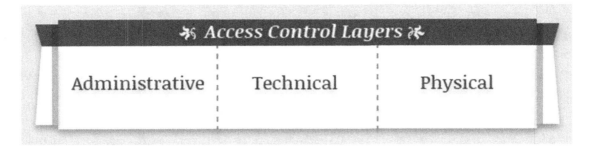

Figure 14-9. *Access Control Layers*

1. **Administrative**: The administrative layer includes policies. Senior management provides the skeleton of a security infrastructure and then appoints the proper entities to fill the rest in. Types of administrative controls include

   - **Policy and Procedures**: Security policy provides direction for employees/departments—how security should be implemented and followed.

   - **Personnel Controls**: Separation of duties and rotation of duties.

   - **Supervisory Structure**: Each employee reports to a superior, and that superior is responsible for that employee's actions.

   - **Security Awareness**: Training.

   - **Testing**: It is important to test. Ask the question: Do all security controls, mechanisms, and procedures properly support the security policy, goals, and objectives?

2. **Technical**: The technical layer includes logical control like the software tools used to restrict a subject's access to an object. Types of technical controls include

   - **System Access**: Technical control that can enforce access control objectives (Kerberos, RADIUS, Diameter, username/password)

   - **Network Architecture**: IP address ranges and subnets, DMZ

   - **Network Access**: Routers, switches firewalls enforce access restriction into and out of a network

- **Encryption and Protocols**: Protect information as it passes throughout a network

- **Control Zone**: Ensures that confidential information is contained and hinders intruders from accessing it through the airwaves (i.e., extra metallic material in walls)

- **Auditing**: Tracks activity within a network

3. **Physical**: Physical controls must support and work with administrative and technical controls. The physical controls usually involve some sort of barrier: network segregation, perimeter security, computer controls, work area separation, data backups, and cabling.

Access Control Types

Access controls can also be categorized according to type. The six category types are listed. An intrusion detection system would be considered a detective control, whereas a firewall would be considered a preventive control.

- **Preventive**: Avoid undesirable events from occurring.

- **Detective**: Identify undesirable events that have occurred.

- **Corrective**: Correct undesirable events that have occurred.

- **Deterrent**: Discourage security violations.

- **Recovery**: Restore resources and capabilities.

- **Compensative**: Provide alternative to other controls.

Bell–LaPadula Security Model

The Bell–LaPadula security model was utilized by the US Military. Since data confidentiality is a chief concern for the military and is essential to its operations, the Bell-LaPadula security model is designed to address data confidentiality in computer operating systems. The model is especially useful in creating the multilevel security systems that implement the military's hierarchical security scheme, which includes levels of classification such as Unclassified, Confidential, Secret, and Top Secret.

The Bell–LaPadula security model employs both mandatory and discretionary access control mechanisms when implementing its two basic security principles. The first principle is the Simple Security Rule and the second is the *-property (pronounced "star property") principle.

The Simple Security Rule states that no subject (such as a user or program) can read information from an object (file or document) with a security classification higher than that possessed by the subject itself. This means that the system must prevent a user with only a Secret clearance from reading a document labeled Top Secret. This rule is also referred to as the "no-read-up" rule.

The *-property principle states that a subject can write to an object only if its security classification is less than or equal to the object's security classification. Since integrity is not the main goal of the security model, this principle allows users to write to files they cannot view and delete files they are not authorized to access.

See Figure 14-10 for an example of the security classifications allowing subjects to read and or write to an object based on its security classification as previously discussed.

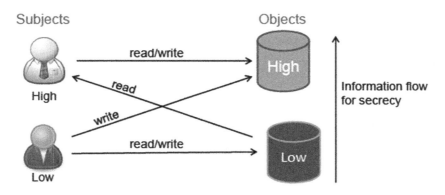

Figure 14-10. *Bell–LaPadula Security Model*

Biba Model

In the Biba security model, instead of security classifications, integrity levels are used. The integrity levels principle is that data with a higher integrity level is believed to be more accurate or reliable than data with a lower integrity level.

Integrity levels indicate the level of trust that can be placed in the information at the different levels. Integrity levels also differ from security classifications as they limit the modification of information as opposed to the flow of information.

High-integrity process

- **High-Integrity Object**: Read and write

- **Low-Integrity Object**: Write

Low-integrity process

- **High-Integrity Object**: Read

- **Low-Integrity Object**: Read and write

See the Biba model illustration in Figure 14-11 which details the process previously described.

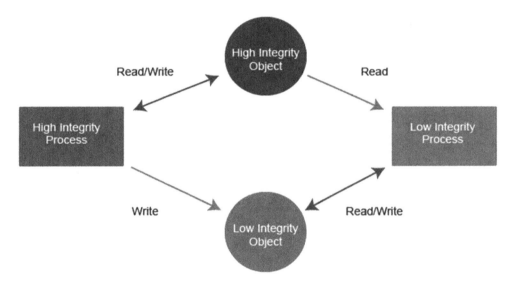

Figure 14-11. *Biba Security Model*

Clark–Wilson Model

The Clark-Wilson security model uses transactions as the basis of its rules. It defines only two levels of integrity: constrained data items (CDI) and unconstrained data items (UDI). CDI data is subject to integrity controls, while UDI data is not. The model then defines two types of processes: integrity verification processes (IVPs) and transformation processes (TPs).

A prime example of an organization using an integrity-based security model would be a financial institution. In the Clark–Wilson security model, the account balance of the banking account would be a CDI because its integrity is a critical function of the bank. A client's color preference of debit card is not a critical function to the bank and would be considered an UDI. Since the integrity of account balances is of extreme importance, changes to a person's balance must be done through the use of a TP. Ensuring the balance is correct would be done by an IVP. Only certain employees of the bank would have the ability to modify a bank account, which would be controlled by limiting the number of individuals who have the authority to execute TPs that result in account modification.

Accountability

Every individual who works with an information system has specific responsibilities for information assurance. The tasks that are a part of these responsibilities are part of the overall information security plan and can be measured by an administrator. A few of the tools used to track specific user responsibilities include

- Track bad deeds back to individuals.

- Detect intrusions.

- Reconstruct events and system conditions.

- Provide legal recourse material.

- Produce problem reports.

Auditing

There are a number of different audits that can be performed at an organization. When performing a logical security audit, for example, the auditor should look at the security controls that are in place. Does the company have a password policy? Are employees aware of proper log-on/log-off procedures?

Keystroke monitoring with a keylogger is another type of audit technology. For example, I may suspect that one of my employees is using company time to run their own website company. I can install keylogger hardware or keylogger software to record that individual's keystrokes which would provide the documentation that I might need to take action against that employee.

Audit logs can be reviewed to provide a chronological record of system activities. It is also important to protect these log files especially if they will be used to prove the guilt of an offending party.

System-Level Events

The operating system on your computer has the capabilities of logging different events. With the Windows operating systems, Event Viewer can be used to view the log files that record the events listed. For example, Windows 7 has the following Windows logs: Application, Security, and System. There are also numerous Applications and Services Log files:

- System performance
- Log-in attempts (successful/unsuccessful)
- Log-on ID
- Date and time of each log-on attempt
- Lockouts of users and terminals
- Use of administrative utilities
- Devices used
- Functions performed
- Requests to alter configuration files

Application-Level Events

Application-level events are also recorded in the log file. The application log in event viewer can be viewed to monitor warnings, errors, files opened and closed, modification of files, security violations within application, or other informational messages.

User-Level Events

User-level events can be initiated by enabling the auditing feature available as a policy setting in the operating system. It is important to take a look at the log files when you are monitoring system events. You can view

- Identification and authentication attempts

- Files, services, and resources used

- Commands initiated

- Security violations

Unauthorized Disclosure of Information

Loss, misuse, or unauthorized access to sensitive information can result in adverse consequences for an individual or organization.

Within an organization, object reuse and emanations and both pose a threat. Object reuse can be found with physical media. Care must be taken to ensure that when an object such as a hard drive is reused, no residual data remains. Object reuse can also refer to the allocation of system resources (storage objects) to a subject. For example, the controlled sharing of memory on a system is more difficult to manage.

Depending on the type of organization, emanations may also be a security concern.

Internal Controls

There are several administrative controls that can be implemented in an organization. Several of those are listed in Figure 14-12.

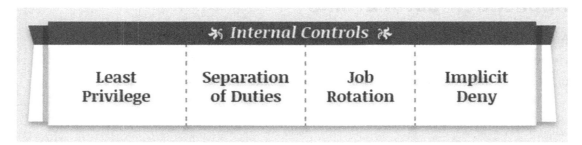

Figure 14-12. *Internal Controls*

Least Privilege

- A subject (user, application, or process) should have only the necessary rights and privileges to perform its task with no additional permissions.

Separation of Duties

- For any given task, more than one individual needs to be involved.

- Applicable to physical environments as well as network and host security.

- No single individual can abuse the system.

- Potential drawbacks are cost, time, and money.

Job Rotation

- The rotation of individuals through different tasks and duties

- Prevents a single point of failure

Implicit Deny

- If a situation is not covered by any of the rules, then access cannot be granted.

- Any individual without proper authorization cannot be granted access.

Policies and Procedures

A policy is the foundation upon which procedures and guidelines are developed. A security policy lays the foundation for the organization's goals for security. Policies will be updated less frequently than the procedures used to implement them.

Security Policy: High-level statement that outlines both what security means to the organization and the organization's goals for security

Procedures: General step-by-step instructions that dictate exactly how employees are expected to act in a given situation or to accomplish a specific task

Guidelines: Suggests the best way to accomplish tasks

Example Policy

The sample policy shown in Figure 14-13 includes the sections which need to be included. All policies should be reviewed on a regular basis and updated as required. Policies should also be reviewed by the organization's legal department, and a plan should be adopted for making the employees aware of the policies.

Subsection	6.1 PERSONNEL SECURITY Change Control #: 1.0	
Policy	6.1.3 Confidentiality Agreements Approved by: SMH	
Objectives	Confidentiality of organizational data is a key tenet of our information security program. In support of this goal, ABC Co will require signed confidentiality agreements of all authorized users of information systems. This agreement shall conform to all federal, state, regulatory, and union requirements.	
Purpose	The purpose of this policy is to protect the assets of the organization by clearly informing staff of their roles and responsibilities for keeping the organization's information confidential.	
Audience	ABC Co confidentiality agreement policy applies equally to all individuals granted access privileges to an ABC Co Information resources	
Policy	This policy requires that staff sign a confidentiality policy agreement prior to being granted access to any sensitive information or systems. Agreements will be reviewed with the staff member when there is any change to the employment or contract, or prior to leaving the organization. The agreements will be provided to the employees by the Human Resource Dept.	
Exceptions	At the discretion of the Information Security Officer, third parties whose contracts include a confidentiality clause may be exempted from signing individual confidentiality agreements.	
Disciplinary Actions	Violation of this policy may result in disciplinary actions, which may include termination for employees and temporaries; a termination of employment relations in the case of contractors or consultants; or dismissal for interns and volunteers. Additionally, individuals are subject to civil and criminal prosecution.	

Figure 14-13. *A Sample Policy with All Necessary Sections*

Acceptable Use Policy

An acceptable use policy (AUP) outlines what the organization considers to be the appropriate use of company resources, such as computer systems, email, Internet usage, and networks. AUP documents reduce the potential for legal action that may be taken by a user. New employees sign an AUP before they are given access to information systems.

The goal of AUP is to ensure employee productivity while limiting organizational liability through inappropriate use of the organization's assets. The AUP clearly dictates which activities are not allowed and addresses the issues of using company resources to conduct personal business, installation of new hardware or software, remote access to systems and networks, the copying of company-owned software, and the responsibility of users to protect company assets including data and hardware or software. Statements regarding possible penalties for infractions should be included.

Additional Security Policies

An Email Usage Policy details whether nonwork email traffic is allowed at all or severely restricted, the types of messages considered appropriate or inappropriate, and any disclaimers that must be attached to an employee's message sent to an individual outside the company.

Considerations for an Email Usage Policy are listed here:

- **Email Usage**: Addresses what the company will allow employees to send in terms of email.

- **Due Care**: Details how employees are expected to treat equipment and data.

- **Need to Know and Least Privilege**: The individual will be granted only the bare minimum number of privileges needed to perform her job.

- **Disposal and Destruction**: Outline the methods for destroying discarded sensitive information.

- **Change Management**: Ensures proper procedures are followed when changes to the IT infrastructure are made.

- **Separation of Duties**: No single individual has the ability to conduct transactions alone.

- **Password Management**: Addresses the procedures used for selecting user passwords, the frequency with which they must be changed, and how they will be distributed as well as procedures should an employee forget her old password.

- **Due Diligence**: Ensures that all options were considered in the development of security policies and procedures related to due care directives.

- **Due Process**: Guarantees fundamental fairness, justice, and liberty in relation to an individual's rights.

There are numerous other security policies. You can find information security policy templates at the SANS website.

Human Resources Policies

As previously discussed, people are the weakest link in the security chain. Therefore, specific policies need to be developed regarding new hires, employee termination, mandatory vacation, and an employee review process.

Summary

In this chapter you learned about privilege management, password policy components, and security controls and permissions. You also reviewed the components relating to access control and policies and procedures useful for implementing appropriate security controls for effective account management.

Resources

- **SANS**: www.sans.org/

- **Security Policy Templates**: www.sans.org/security-resources/
  policies/

CHAPTER 15

Cryptography

In this chapter you will learn about several methods of cryptography that were used in ancient Greece. You will also examine encryption algorithms used today and how you can apply encryption to maintain two of the three security principles—confidentiality and integrity.

By the end of this chapter, you will be able to

1. Summarize general cryptography concepts.

2. Apply appropriate cryptographic tools and products.

Cryptography

Cryptography is the science of taking plain, readable text and applying an algorithm to it, encrypting it to create ciphertext, which appears to be gibberish until it is decrypted. Encryption is used to maintain confidentiality. Cryptography itself is not a modern technology.

Keys: A key is used by an algorithm to encrypt or decrypt a message. The key is an important component in the encryption algorithm. An algorithm is only as good as the key being used. The more complexity involved, the more secure the algorithm is. Key management is an issue that needs to be addressed since the key is such an important component in the process.

Shift Cipher: The shift cipher is a substitution cipher that uses an offset (which is the key) to shift the second alphabet forward or backward. Using the shift cipher pictured in Figure 15-1, can you figure out what the key is? Take the plaintext and security, and apply the algorithm to come up with the ciphertext.

© Ahmed F. Sheikh 2020

A. F Sheikh, *CompTIA Security+ Certification Study Guide*, https://doi.org/10.1007/978-1-4842-6234-4_15

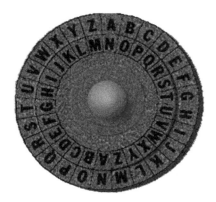

Figure 15-1. *Graphic Representation of a Caesar Cipher*

Substitution Cipher: A substitution cipher like the shift cipher was easy to crack. All you have to do is look for patterns and letters that appear in multiple words. Substitution ciphers work on the principle of substituting a different letter for every letter, for instance, a becomes g, and b becomes d. The letters are not in order as they are in shift ciphers.

Vigenère Cipher: The Vigenère cipher is a polyalphabetic cipher based on substitution using multiple substitution alphabets. A password is still used. A table (see Figure 15-2), a portion of which is shown, is also used. The intersection of the first letter in the password and the first letter of the plaintext phrase is the ciphertext used to represent our plaintext letter. If the password is not as long as the phrase, the password is repeated.

```
  A B C D E F G H I J K L M N O P Q R S T U V W X Y Z
A A B C D E F G H I J K L M N O P Q R S T U V W X Y Z
B B C D E F G H I J K L M N O P Q R S T U V W X Y Z A
C C D E F G H I J K L M N O P Q R S T U V W X Y Z A B
D D E F G H I J K L M N O P Q R S T U V W X Y Z A B C
E E F G H I J K L M N O P Q R S T U V W X Y Z A B C D
F F G H I J K L M N O P Q R S T U V W X Y Z A B C D E
G G H I J K L M N O P Q R S T U V W X Y Z A B C D E F
H H I J K L M N O P Q R S T U V W X Y Z A B C D E F G
I I J K L M N O P Q R S T U V W X Y Z A B C D E F G H
J J K L M N O P Q R S T U V W X Y Z A B C D E F G H I
K K L M N O P Q R S T U V W X Y Z A B C D E F G H I J
L L M N O P Q R S T U V W X Y Z A B C D E F G H I J K
M M N O P Q R S T U V W X Y Z A B C D E F G H I J K L
N N O P Q R S T U V W X Y Z A B C D E F G H I J K L M
O O P Q R S T U V W X Y Z A B C D E F G H I J K L M N
P P Q R S T U V W X Y Z A B C D E F G H I J K L M N O
Q Q R S T U V W X Y Z A B C D E F G H I J K L M N O P
R R S T U V W X Y Z A B C D E F G H I J K L M N O P Q
S S T U V W X Y Z A B C D E F G H I J K L M N O P Q R
T T U V W X Y Z A B C D E F G H I J K L M N O P Q R S
U U V W X Y Z A B C D E F G H I J K L M N O P Q R S T
V V W X Y Z A B C D E F G H I J K L M N O P Q R S T U
W W X Y Z A B C D E F G H I J K L M N O P Q R S T U V
X X Y Z A B C D E F G H I J K L M N O P Q R S T U V W
Y Y Z A B C D E F G H I J K L M N O P Q R S T U V W X
Z Z A B C D E F G H I J K L M N O P Q R S T U V W X Y
```

Figure 15-2. *A Vigenère Table Can Be Used for Encryption or Decryption*

The key in this encryption system is still the password. This algorithm is simple, but it still provides strong security. Even if someone knows about the table, they do not know the key, or password, so the message cannot be decrypted.

One-Time Pad: The one-time pad is almost impossible to crack. The name comes from the fact that two identical pads of paper containing the key material were used. The top sheet could be torn off and destroyed after it was used. The encrypted message provides no information about the original message. The problem is that the one-time pad requires perfectly random key material which is the challenge with a modern-day application. The key exchange is also an issue.

A one-time pad is unbreakable, dependent on random pad generation, and requires both parties to have the identical pad and that they start at the same point in the pad. The need to have both parties to have the identical pad and start from the same point in the pad is impractical for most common applications for reasons such as these large pads may be required, it is difficult to generate truly random numbers, and it is difficult to get the pads to both parties.

Common Uses of Hashing Functions

Hashing functions are used to ensure that a message or data has not changed. In other words, we are talking about maintaining integrity. If you download a program from the Internet, you may see that a message digest value is noted using a particular hashing algorithm. After you download the file, use a hash calculator on that file. Your result should be an exact match to the value provided at the website. If the values are not the same, it means that the file has been tampered with in some way.

Hash Algorithms

Two widely used hash algorithms are SHA and Message Digest. There are also numerous tools available on the Internet that you can use to calculate hash values for files or character strings.

SHA

Applies compression function to data input

- Accepts up to 2^{64} bits or less and then compresses it down to a smaller number of bits (i.e., 160 bits for SHA-1)

Longer versions are referred to as SHA-2:

- SHA-256, SHA-384, and SHA-512.

- Longer hash results mean more difficult to attack successfully.

- SHAKE-128 and SHAKE-256 are introduced in the latest hashing algorithm SHA-3.

Message Digest (MD)

MD5[1]

- Creates a 128-bit hash of a message of any length and segments the message into 512-bit blocks

Symmetric Encryption

Having the same key is the basis for even the oldest ciphers. In shift ciphers both parties need to know the direction and amount of shift being performed. All symmetric algorithms are based upon this shared secret principle, including the unbreakable one-time pad method. And, as was previously mentioned, the challenge with these methods is the mechanism used for key management. A cryptographic key is involved in symmetric encryption, so there must be a mechanism for key management. See Figure 15-3.

---

[1]http://searchsecurity.techtarget.com/definition/MD5

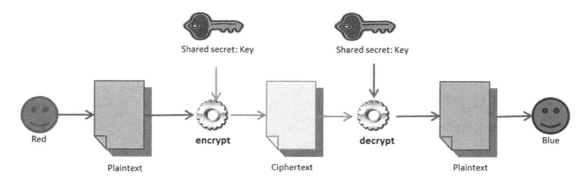

Figure 15-3. *Cryptographic Public and Private Keys Being Used to Encrypt and Decrypt*

Key Management

Keys must be managed at all stages. That requires securing it on the local computer, securing it on the remote system, protecting it from data corruption, protecting it from loss, and, probably the most important step, protecting it while it is transmitted between the two parties. For symmetric algorithms, the most important lesson is to store and send the key only by a known, secure means. Public key cryptography greatly eases the key management issue.

Trusted Platform Module (TPM)

The Trusted Platform Module provides a hardware-based key storage location that can be used by many applications. Combining hardware with software provides better security than a software-only solution. To learn more, review "Windows Trusted Platform Module Management Step-by-Step Guide."[2]

Symmetric Algorithms

You should be familiar with the various symmetric algorithms and their main characteristics. Most of the algorithms listed are block ciphers, which means that they operate on a fixed-length group of bits with a fixed, unvarying transformation. If the length of the plaintext message is not a multiple of the length of a block, the plaintext

---

[2]http://technet.microsoft.com/en-us/library/cc749022(v=WS.10).aspx

message must be padded. A stream cipher applies a cryptographic key and algorithm to each binary digit in a data stream and can encrypt plaintext messages of variable length. Please see the following details regarding the various symmetric algorithms and their main characteristics.

Data Encryption Standard (DES)

- Block cipher
- The block size is 64-, 56-bit key length

Triple Data Encryption Standard (3DES)

- Uses either two or three keys
- Multiple encryption— goes through the DES algorithm three times

Advanced Encryption Standard (AES)

- Block cipher that separates data input into 128-, 192-, or 256-bit blocks
- Key sizes of 128, 192, and 256 bits, with the size of the key affecting the number of rounds used in the algorithm

Carlisle Adams and Stafford Tavares (CAST)

- Uses 64-bit block size for 64- and 128-bit keys
- 128-bit block size for the 256-bit key version

RC6

- 128-bit block size, keys sizes: 128, 192, 256
- Runs well on 32-bit computers and resistant to brute force attacks

RC4

- Stream cipher
- Uses key lengths of 8 to 2048 bits, most vulnerable to possibility of weak keys

Blowfish

- Block mode cipher, using 64-bit blocks and a variable key length from 32 to 448 bits
- Runs well on 32-bit machines

International Data Encryption Algorithm (IDEA)

- Block mode cipher using 64-bit block size and 128-bit key

Asymmetric Encryption

Asymmetric encryption is also known as public key encryption. This method relies on having a key pair—the public key and a private key. The two keys are mathematically related, but you cannot figure out the private key just because you know someone's public key.

A key pair gets generated. The public key gets published to a third-party server where others will be able to access it. A user's private key stays with the user (e.g., within the software application). One key locks or encrypts the plaintext, and the other unlocks or decrypts the ciphertext. Neither key can perform both functions by itself. The public key may be published without compromising security, while the private key must not be revealed to anyone not authorized to read the messages.

For example, say you needed to send Blue an encrypted message. You would use Blue's public key, accessed via a third-party server, to encrypt the message, and then you would send it to her. Blue would use her private key to decrypt the message. Even if Green intercepted the message, he would not be able to decrypt the message even though he also has access to Blue's public key. See Figure 15-4 for illustration.

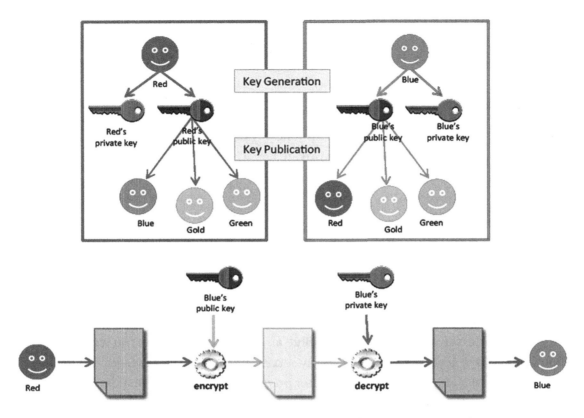

Figure 15-4. *How to Encrypt a Message Based on the Given Example*

Asymmetric Algorithms

Several of the asymmetric algorithms are listed along with how they are applied. See Figure 15-5.

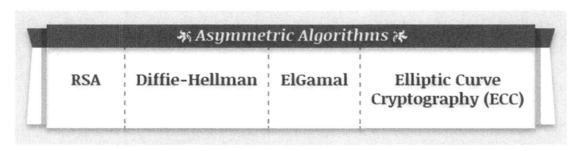

Figure 15-5. *Asymmetric Algorithms*

RSA: Used for encryption and digital signatures; uses the product of two very large prime numbers (between 100 and 200 digits long and of equal length)

Diffie–Hellman: Electronic key exchange method of the Secure Sockets Layer (SSL) protocol; TLS, SSH, and IPsec protocols; enables the sharing of a secret key

ElGamal: This system was never patented and is free for use; used as the US government standard for digital signatures

Elliptic Curve Cryptography (ECC): Works on the basis of elliptic curves

Steganography

Steganography is the method of hiding data (the message) in another file. Data can be hidden in graphic, audio, or other text files. The advantage of steganography over cryptography is that the message does not attract any special attention. You would never know that a picture actually contained a secret message by viewing the file either electronically or in hard copy.

Cryptography Algorithm Use: Confidentiality

Maintaining confidentiality often is important for both stored data and transmitted data. In both cases, symmetric encryption is favored because of its speed and because some asymmetric algorithms can significantly increase the size of the object being encrypted.

In the case of a stored item, a public key is typically unnecessary, as the item is being encrypted to protect it from access by others. In the case of transmitted data, public key cryptography is typically used to exchange the secret key, and then symmetric cryptography is used to ensure the confidentiality of the data being sent.

Asymmetric cryptography does protect confidentiality, but its size and speed make it more efficient at protecting the confidentiality of small units for tasks such as electronic key exchange. In all cases, the strength of the algorithms and the length of the keys ensure the secrecy of the data in question. Please review the following aspects of "Cryptography Algorithm Use: Confidentiality."

Confidentiality

- Encryption excels at providing confidentiality.

- Maintains confidentiality on data stored or transmitted.

Integrity

- Crucial component of message security.

- The hash functions compute the message digests, and this guarantees the integrity of the message.

Nonrepudiation

- The message sender cannot later deny that they sent the message.

- This is important in electronic exchanges of data.

Authentication

- Allows you to prove you are who you say you are

Key Escrow

- Keeps a copy of the encryption key with a trusted third party

Cryptography Algorithm Use: Digital Signatures

Unprotected digital documents are very easy for anyone to change. If a document is edited after an individual signs it, it is important that any modification can be detected.

To protect against document editing, hashing functions are used to create a digest of the message that is unique and easily reproducible by both parties. This ensures that the message integrity is complete. See Figure 15-6.

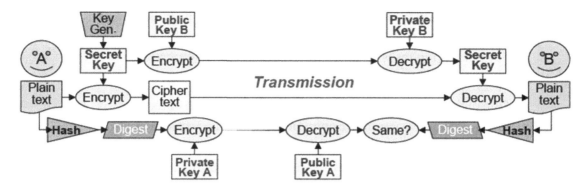

Figure 15-6. *Graphic Representation of Hashing Functions and Asymmetric Cryptography Used to Create Digital Signatures*

Cryptography Algorithm Use: Digital Rights Management (DRM)

Digital rights management, or DRM, is the process for protecting intellectual property from unauthorized use. DRM is used by hardware manufacturers, publishers, and individuals that want to limit the use of digital content after it has been sold. Those who are for the technology argue that it is necessary to fight copyright infringement. Those opposed say it restricts them from performing legal tasks such as making a backup copy.

Cryptographic Applications

It is important to be aware of the various types of cryptographic applications shown in Figure 15-7.

❧ Cryptographic Applications ❧				
Pretty Good Privacy (PGP)	TrueCrypt	FreeOTFE	GnuPG, or Gnu Privacy Guard	BitLocker

Figure 15-7. *Cryptographic Applications*

1. **Pretty Good Privacy (PGP)**: PGP applications can be plugged into popular email programs to handle the majority of day-to-day encryption tasks using a combination of symmetric and asymmetric encryption protocols.

   One of the unique features of PGP is its ability to use both symmetric and asymmetric encryption methods, accessing the strengths of each method and avoiding the weaknesses of each as well. Symmetric keys are used for bulk encryption, taking advantage of the speed and efficiency of symmetric encryption. The symmetric keys are passed using asymmetric methods, capitalizing on the flexibility of this method.

2. **TrueCrypt**: *TrueCrypt* is an open source solution for encryption. It is designed for symmetric disk-based encryption of your files. It features Advanced Encryption Standard (AES) ciphers and the ability to create a *deniable volume*, encryption stored within encryption so that volume cannot be reliably detected. TrueCrypt can perform file encryption and whole disk encryption. Whole disk encryption encrypts the entire hard drive of a computer, including the operating system.

3. **FreeOTFE**: *FreeOTFE* is similar to TrueCrypt. It offers "on-the-fly" disk encryption as an open source, freely downloadable application. It can encrypt files up to entire disks with several popular ciphers, including AES.

4. **GnuPG**: *GnuPG*, or *Gnu Privacy Guard*, is an open source implementation of the OpenPGP standard. This command line-based tool is a public key encryption program designed to protect electronic communications such as email. It operates similarly to PGP and includes a method for managing public/private keys.

   File system encryption is becoming a standard means of protecting data while in storage. Even hard drives are available with built-in AES encryption. Microsoft introduced BitLocker, its Encrypting File System (EFS).

5. **BitLocker**: BitLocker is a boot sector encryption method that protects data on the latest Windows operating systems. BitLocker utilizes AES encryption to encrypt every file on the hard drive automatically. All encryption occurs in the background, and decryption occurs seamlessly when data is requested. The decryption key can be stored in the Trusted Platform Module (TPM) or on a Universal Serial Bus (USB) key.

Summary

In this chapter you learned about fundamental concepts relating to cryptography. You reviewed the basics of cryptography and the common uses of hashing functions, symmetric encryption, symmetric algorithms, and asymmetric algorithms. In this chapter, you also became familiar with cryptography as used for exchanging information which requires confidentiality and the use of digital signatures. This chapter highlighted various cryptographic tools and products that can be implemented to maintain confidentiality and integrity which are two of the three security principles.

Resource

- **MD5**: http://searchsecurity.techtarget.com/definition/MD5

CHAPTER 16

Public Key Infrastructure

Public key infrastructure (PKI) includes elements required to manage digital certificates. In this chapter, you will learn about the various components involved with public key infrastructure and trusted relationships.

By the end of this chapter, you will be able to

1. Explain the core concepts of public key infrastructure.

2. Implement public key infrastructure (PKI), certificate management, and associated components.

Public Key Infrastructure

Public key infrastructure, or PKI, includes the hardware, software, policies, and procedures required to manage digital certificates. Consider that two parties want to communicate securely with the additional requirement that they are sure with whom they are actually interacting with. PKI uses a trusted third party to vouch for the credentials of the parties involved.

If you have ever applied for a passport, the same concept applies. You fill out the application, and a third party validates it and issues the passport. To use your passport to travel between countries, it must be valid. The country that you are entering is going to make sure that your passport has not been revoked.

Certificate Authorities (CA)

The certificate authority, or CA, is the entity that certifies the identities of the parties involved and creates a digital certificate so that either party can be sure of whom they are communicating with. Digital certificates establish an association between the subject's identity and a public key. RSA, Verisign, and Thawte are considered to be reputable public CAs.

© Ahmed F. Sheikh 2020
A. F Sheikh, *CompTIA Security+ Certification Study Guide*, https://doi.org/10.1007/978-1-4842-6234-4_16

Certification practices statement (CPS) outlines how identities are verified. A certificate server is the service that issues certificates. The service constructs the digital certificate and combines the user's public key with the resulting certificate. The certificate is then digitally signed with the CA's private key.

Registration Authorities (RA)

The registration authority, or RA, verifies the identity of the certificate requestor on behalf of the CA. The CA generates the certificate using information forwarded by the RA. The authentication requirements differ depending on the type of certificate being requested. Most CAs offer a series of classes for certificates with increasing trust by class. If an application creates a key store that can be accessed by other applications, it will provide a standardized interface, called the application programing interface (API).

Steps for Obtaining a Digital Certificate

The certificate authority owns a certificate server. The certificate authority has the certificate server issue a certificate, digitally signed with the certificate authority's private key:

1.   User registers for a digital certificate.

2.   Random values determined.

3.   Algorithm generates a public/private key pair.

4.   Key pair is stored in a key store on the workstation.

5.   Copy of public key is sent to the CA.

6.   The CA generates a digital certificate containing the public key.

7.   New certificate is sent to user.

See Figure 16-1 for an example.

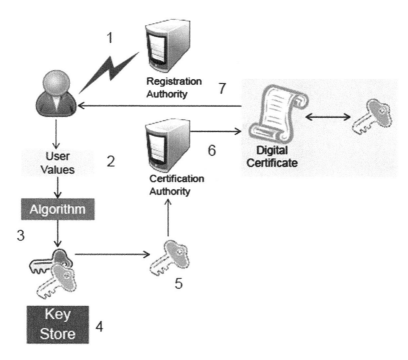

Figure 16-1. *Steps for Obtaining a Digital Certificate*

Trust and Certificate Verification

The trusted third party vouches for the other individual before confidence can be instilled and sensitive communication can take place. When a user trusts a CA, they will download that CA's digital certificate and public key, which will be stored on their local computer. Most browsers have a list of CAs configured to be trusted by default, so when a user installs a new web browser, several of the most well-known and most trusted CAs will be trusted without any change of settings. See Figures 16-2 and 16-3.

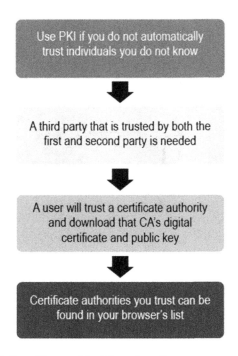

Figure 16-2. *Trust and Certificate Verification Process*

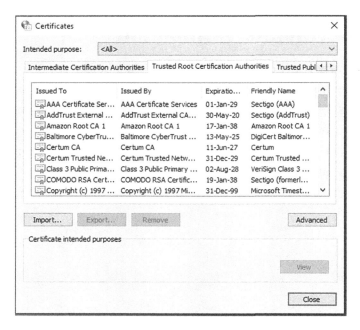

Figure 16-3. *Certificates Screen Showing the List of Trusted Root Certification Authorities*

Digital Certificates

The X.509 is the standard and specifies standard formats for certificates and certificate revocation lists. You can go to the browser and view a digital certificate. For Internet Explorer, go to Internet Options, and select the Content Tab. Click the Certificates button. See Figure 16-4. For details on certificates, visit the International Telecommunication Union.[1]

Figure 16-4. *Certificate Window with the Details Tab Highlighted*

---

[1]www.itu.int/en/Pages/default.aspx

Revocation

A certificate cannot be assumed to be valid without checking for revocation before each use. For example, a certificate, which is bound to a user's key pair, identifies the user as an employee of the company. If the administrator wants to ensure that the key pair could not be used in the future to validate this person's affiliation with the company, he would revoke the certificate.

There are several reasons that a certificate might be revoked:

- A user may have lost a laptop or a smart card that stored a private key.

- An improper software implementation may have been uncovered that directly affected the security of a private key.

- A user may have fallen victim to a social engineering attack and inadvertently given up a private key.

- Data held within the certificate may no longer apply to the specified individual.

- An employee may leave a company and should not be identified as a member of an in-house PKI any longer.

Once revoked, a certificate cannot be reinstated. This is to prevent an unauthorized reinstatement by someone who has unauthorized access to the key(s). A key pair can be reinstated for use by issuing a new certificate if at a later time the keys are found to be secure. The old certificate would still be void, but the new one would be valid. The CA provides the following type of protection by maintaining a certificate revocation list (CRL):

- A list of serial numbers of certificates that have been revoked

- A statement indicating why the individual certificates were revoked and a date when the revocation took place

Key Recovery

Key archiving is the process of storing a set of keys to be used as a backup. If something happens to the original set, the backup keys can be used for key recovery. Requiring two individuals to recover a lost key together is called dual control, which simply means that two people have to be present to carry out a specific task. Dual control supports the principle of *separation of duties*, which means that one person cannot complete a critical task by himself.

M of N Authentication

Using m of n authentication schemes can improve security by requiring that multiple people perform critical functions preventing a single party from compromising a secret.

M of N Authentication   *n* number of people can be involved in the key recovery process, but at least *m* (which is a smaller number than *n*) *must* be involved before the task can be completed.

For example, a company would not require all possible individuals to be involved in the recovery process, because getting all the people together at the same time could be impossible considering meetings, vacations, sick time, and travel. At least some of all possible individuals must be available to participate, and this is the subset *m* of the number *n*.

Requiring too many people for the *m* subset increases issues associated with availability, whereas requiring too few increases the risk of a small number of people colluding to compromise a secret.

Key Escrow

Key escrow is a process of giving keys to a third party so that they can decrypt and read sensitive information when this need arises. Key escrow is a controversial topic. The security of the escrowed key is a concern, and it needs to be managed at the same security level as the original key. Key escrow almost always pertains to handing over encryption keys to the government, or to another higher authority, so that the keys can be used to collect evidence during investigations.

Trust Models

A trust domain is the systems, personnel, applications, protocols, technologies, and policies that work together to provide a level of protection. Three trust models exist: hierarchical, peer to peer, and hybrid. Hierarchical trust is like an upside-down tree; peer to peer is a lateral series of references; and hybrid is a combination of hierarchical and peer-to-peer trust.

Summary

In this chapter you learned about the basic concepts of public key infrastructure. You reviewed the steps for obtaining a digital certificate, key recovery, and trust models. You learned about the importance of implementing a public key infrastructure to manage digital certificates.

Resource

- **International Telecommunication Union**: www.itu.int/en/Pages/ default.aspx

Index

A

Access control
  administrative layer, 226
  lists, 224
  physical layer, 227
  technical layer, 226
  types, 227
Accountability, 230
Annual loss expectancy (ALE), 79
Anti-spam software, 60
Antivirus solutions, 56
  automated scanning, 56
  automated updates, 56
  email scanning, 57
  heuristic scanning, 58
  manual scanning, 57
  media scanning, 56
  resolution, 57
  signature based scanning, 57
Application-level events, 231
Asymmetric algorithms, 244
Attacks, 141
  avenue of, 141
  on encryption, 144
  injection attack, 145
  malicious code, 145
  malware defense, 146
  minimizing possible avenues, 142
  password attack, 144
  pharming, 144
  phishing, 143
  social engineering, 148
  software exploitation, 145
  systems and networks, 143
  types of, 5
  war-dialing, 147
  war-driving, 148
Auditing, 230, 231
Authentication and remote access, 201
  accounting, 202
  authentication, 202
  authorization, 202

B

Baselines, 163, 164
Bell–LaPadula security model, 227, 228
Biba security model, 228
Bluetooth vulnerabilities, 38
Business continuity plan (BCP), 98
  backup plan, 99, 100
  cold Site, 101
  hot Site, 101
  secure recovery, 102
  utilities, 101
  warm Site, 101

C

Certification and Accreditation (C&A), 82
  agreements, 84
  approval to operate, 83

© Ahmed F. Sheikh 2020
A. F Sheikh, *CompTIA Security+ Certification Study Guide*, https://doi.org/10.1007/978-1-4842-6234-4

Printed in the United States
By Bookmasters